Other Books by Richard J. Barnet

THE LEAN YEARS: Politics in the Age of Scarcity

THE GIANTS: Russia and America

GLOBAL REACH: The Power of the Multinational Corporations
(with Ronald E. Müller)

ROOTS OF WAR: The Men and Institutions Behind U.S. Foreign
Policy

THE ECONOMY OF DEATH

INTERVENTION AND REVOLUTION

AFTER TWENTY YEARS (with Marcus G. Raskin)

WHO WANTS DISARMAMENT?

Real Security

Restoring American Power in a Dangerous Decade

by Richard J. Barnet

A TOUCHSTONE BOOK

PUBLISHED BY SIMON AND SCHUSTER, NEW YORK

A Touchstone Book
Published by Simon and Schuster
A Division of Gulf & Western Corporation
Simon & Schuster Building
Rockefeller Center
1230 Avenue of the Americas
New York New York 10020
TOUCHSTONE and colophon are trademarks of Simon & Schuster
Designed by Irving Perkins and Associates
Manufactured in the United States of America
10 9 8 7 6 5 4 3

Library of Congress Cataloging in Publication Data

Barnet, Richard J.
    Real security.

    Bibliography: p.
    Includes index.
    1. United States—National security.   2. United
States—Military policy.   I. Title.
UA23.B335   355'.033073   81-4502
                                        AACR2
ISBN 0-671-43172-2
0-671-43166-8 Pbk.

Significant portions of this book appeared originally in slightly
altered form in *The New Yorker, Foreign Affairs* and *Christianity
and Crisis.*

FOR GORDON COSBY AND BILL PRICE

Acknowledgments

I wish to thank Peter Kornbluh, Carol Benke, and Nancy Ameen for research assistance and other contributions to this book.

Contents

CHAPTER 1

What Happened to the American Century?

Americans' perceptions of their nation's power have changed radically in the last five years. Until the withdrawal from Vietnam and the collapse of the Nixon-Kissinger vision of détente, it scarcely occurred to anyone that the United States was declining in influence. "We are the number one nation," President Lyndon B. Johnson told the National Foreign Policy Conference at the State Department at a crucial moment in the Vietnam War, "and we are going to stay the number one nation." Today it is commonplace to hear that the "military balance" is shifting to the Soviet Union. The "Vietnam Syndrome"—a reticence about using military power abroad for fear of becoming bogged down in another divisive war—is widely regarded as the reason other nations, including allies, former allies, and adversaries, are becoming increasingly bold in opposing our interests or pursuing their own.

Since 1975 a number of U.S. ambassadors have been kidnapped or murdered. Embassies have been sacked. A handful of Iranian students managed to humiliate the United

States for over a year by holding fifty-two of her diplomats hostage. "The spectacle of a Mexican President lecturing the President of the United States," as U.S. banker S. A. Constance characterized Jimmy Carter's encounter with López Portillo in February 1979, epitomizes the "erosion of American power." The judgment that the U.S. has become a "crippled giant," to use Senator William S. Cohen's phrase, is widespread. For such observers, the decline in American power is symbolized by the battles the nation refused to join: the victorious fight of left-wing forces in Angola, Nicaragua, and Ethiopia, the overthrow of America's "friend," Mohammed Reza Shah Pahlavi, and the Soviet invasion of Afghanistan. "The overall military balance is shifting sharply against us," Henry Kissinger told the American Society of Newspaper Editors in April 1980.

In the mid-1970s, in the wake of the Indochina War, it was fashionable to talk about the need to respect the limits of military power, the necessity of coexistence with the other nuclear superpowers, and the urgency of "global concerns" that transcended the Cold War. The Carter Administration came in with a new post-Vietnam agenda that included normalization of relations with Hanoi and the withdrawal of ground troops from Korea. There were "festering sores that had to be dealt with—Vietnam, Cuba, the Panama Canal," as Secretary of State Vance put it in a *New York Times* interview in May 1977. "The day when we were obsessed by security commitments is over and that strengthens us because it frees us," explained Richard Holbrooke, Assistant Secretary of State for East Asian Affairs. But as the new decade opened, the Carter Administration proposed to spend $1 trillion in five years to redress the military balance. At their convention in Detroit, the Republicans proposed spending a good deal more to restore again the "military superiority" on which U.S. national security rested in the Eisenhower-Kennedy years.

The decline of American power is real. To a considerable extent it is a consequence of inevitable world political and economic developments some of which we encouraged ourselves. To a regrettable extent America's loss of power and loss of confidence is a direct consequence of self-inflicted wounds.

In 1941 Henry Luce coined the term "American Century"; four years later the United States emerged from the Second World War the preeminent power on earth. The catastrophe that brought Hitler's Reich and the Empire of Japan to their knees also brought devastation to America's principal allies. On the day of victory England was bankrupt, French and Italian society had dissolved, and the Russians were still burying their twenty million dead. The catastrophe that had destroyed most of the rest of the industrial world left the United States richer and stronger than ever before. The number-one nation was the world's banker, the sole possessor of the weapon that revolutionized politics, and the only nation capable of projecting its military power to the most distant points on the globe.

The American Century lasted about twenty-six years. Since 1945, three world historic forces have been at work which have over a generation fundamentally altered the power position the United States briefly enjoyed at the end of the war. The first was revolutionary nationalism which brought about the end of the European imperial systems. Decolonization, a process which the United States encouraged at the end of the war, has led to the emergence of a hundred or more new nations. Power has been widely diffused. The world is less neat and much less manageable than in the brief period of the "bipolar" world when reading the newspapers suggested that nothing happened in the world unless the United States or the Soviet Union was behind it.

The second force was the triumph of capitalism in the two defeated Axis powers. The United States played a major role in the recovery of Germany and Japan, and it did so for sound economic and political reasons. Our market-oriented economy could not grow in a world in which the rest of the industrial world was stagnant. A permanently demoralized Germany and Japan would have been a breeding ground for war even if the Soviet Union had not existed. When the Cold War began, the economic and political reintegration of Germany and Japan into the industrial West appeared especially urgent. But the consequence of German and Japanese revival is a loss of American power. Their very existence as economic superpowers limits the autonomy of the United States. We are no longer free to manage our own economy as if other powerful industrial nations did not exist. The world monetary crisis of the 1970s and the decline of the dollar are evidence that we are no longer the sole impresario of the world economy.

The third force that changed America's power position was the arms race. It was inevitable that the Russians would acquire the atomic bomb and that once they did the enviable position the U.S. enjoyed in 1945 would be lost. The Soviet military buildup began in earnest after the Cuban Missile Crisis of 1962. At some point in the late 1960s the Soviet Union achieved the capacity to destroy the United States in a nuclear war even if the United States struck first. The new reality has produced a qualitative change in the relationship between the two superpowers. As Henry Kissinger once put it, the notion of "superiority" now had no meaning. The threat to make nuclear war to advance political interests has become equally absurd for both nations.

There is a widespread view that the decline of American power is attributable to our flagging efforts in the arms race. Alarmist speeches about the "present danger" suggest that if only the U.S. would spend more on the military and use military power more aggressively, the decline in power could be reversed. Yet there is something unconvincing about the argument. The United States has spent almost $3 trillion on national security since 1945. We are less secure today than we were then. Our military expenditures exceed those of all other nations for this period. We are the only nation in the world with a string of hundreds of bases far from our shores. We have more destructive power than any nation on earth has ever had. But we seem unable to translate this awesome array of lethal hardware into political power.

As the 1980s begin, the debate about national security has degenerated into a numbers game. We test reality to see if we are secure by counting all sorts of things. The United States has more bombs than the Russians. But the Soviets have more missiles than the Americans. U.S. missiles are more accurate; Soviet missiles are bigger and more destructive. If you take the last five years, the Soviet Union may well have "outspent" the United States. If you take the last fifteen years, it is clear that the United States has invested far more in the military than has the Soviet Union. What does it all mean? Does it matter?

In looking at national security in the 1980s one must to an extent look at numbers and try to understand what the military forces of the two sides are, what their purposes are, and how they might affect each other. But the larger questions have to do with the nature of military power itself. We are entering an era in which unprecedented limitations on military power now seem to apply. It is not that military power is useless. By no means. Organized violence is still the most persistent and obvious mechanism of political change around the world. But the "hypertrophy of war," as the military writer Walter Millis once put it, has fundamentally altered the relationship between war and politics. The very size and uncontrollability of military operations has seriously undermined their usefulness in the promotion of traditional national-security goals. War itself has become an uncontrollable chain reaction.

Our historical moment is punctuated by the atomic bomb, but it did not begin with the bomb. In 1910 Norman Angell, a British journalist, published *The Great Illusion,* a vastly popular book with a simple and appealing thesis: the interdependence of nations had rendered war obsolete and hence "improbable." The debris of modern war—"commercial disaster, financial ruin and individual suffering"—would so obviously fall on victor and vanquished alike that major military action was now unthinkable.

Scarcely four years later Europe was in flames; in just one month, August 1914, almost 300,000 Frenchmen died. *The Great Illusion* was itself an illusion. Or so it seemed. In fact the World War disproved one part of Angell's thesis and confirmed the other. As prediction it was a piece of naiveté. The prospects of catastrophic war did not turn out to be "pregnant with restraining influences," because the statesmen of Europe resolutely refused to face them. As Barbara Tuchman has so brilliantly shown in *The Guns of August,* they did not mean to go to war at all, and when they did they assumed that the war would be short because no one could afford a long one.

But the financial and economic interdependence of nations, it turned out, defined the new international reality even more decisively than Angell had suggested. The fruits of victory were scarcely distinguishable from the fruits of defeat—the bleeding of a generation, severe economic crisis, and the setting of the stage for a second round. One world war later, Angell's point was even clearer. The nations that started it were in ruins, as indeed were all the victors save one, and that nation, with a monopoly of world power unequalled in all history, was forced for its own economic survival to invest billions in the restoration of the nations that had attacked her, thereby creating formidable commercial rivals.

In the era of nuclear war there are no winners. According

to a 1980 study of the Office of Technology Assessment, a single nuclear weapon landing on Detroit could produce two million casualties immediately and "many" additional deaths from injuries. An attack limited to ten missiles on oil refineries could cause five million immediate deaths plus "cancer deaths in millions." An attack on a range of military and economic targets using a large fraction of the existing arsenal would cause up to 160 million immediate deaths plus tens of millions more who would die because the economy could no longer support them, and millions still more from long-term radiation effects. The happy outcome for the United States in the Second World War cannot be repeated. The circle Norman Angell described in 1910 has now been closed.

CHAPTER 2

In Search of the Military Balance

In the United States, surges of military spending traditionally follow the discovery of gaps between Soviet capabilities and our own. In the early 1950s it was the "bomber gap"; in the Kennedy era, the "missile gap." In the 1970s the discovery of three gaps has dominated the debate on national security: the spending gap, a new and different sort of missile gap, and a "doctrine" gap.

The dollar gap was discovered in 1975 when Secretary of Defense James Schlesinger announced that the Soviets were "outspending us by 50 percent." The following year, the CIA estimates of Russian military spending were doubled overnight because, as a recent Air Force study prepared by the U.S. Strategic Institute puts it, previous estimates had "been in error by as much as 100 percent." In fact the annual growth in Soviet expenditures continued to be steady and relatively modest. Between 1964 and 1974 the annual rate of growth in Soviet military expenditures averaged 2.7 percent. According to a 1980 CIA estimate, Soviet defense activities in the 1970–79 period "increased at an average annual rate of 3 per cent." From 1964 to 1968, U.S. military

16

spending increased, but with the beginning of the withdrawal from Vietnam the Pentagon budget declined about one percent a year for five successive years. This trend had already been reversed by the end of the Vietnam War.

The dramatic new estimates were not based on the discovery of new or accelerated Soviet building programs, but on new ways of calculating the burden of defense expenditures on the Soviet economy. Instead of spending 6 or 8 percent of the gross national product on defense, the military sector was taking almost twice as much of the national wealth as previously believed. According to a 1976 CIA report, "The new estimate of the share of defense in the Soviet GNP . . . does not mean that the impact of defense programs on the Soviet economy has increased—only that our appreciation of this impact has changed. It also implies that Soviet defense industries are far less efficient than formerly believed." In 1980, the CIA calculated that Soviet military spending was increasing 4 to 5 percent a year even though the economy as a whole "slowed to a crawl."

The spending-gap controversy illustrates some of the Alice-in-Wonderland aspects of the arms race. American insecurity rises with the dollars we impute to the Soviet military effort. But in fact actual Soviet expenditures are not known. The U.S. intelligence community reconstructs the Soviet military budget by asking, "What would it cost to buy the Soviet defense establishment in the United States at U.S. prices?" Our intelligence analysts pretend that the Soviets procure their tanks from General Motors and that they pay U.S. volunteer wages to their conscripts. "By computing Soviet manpower costs at U.S. rates," Congressman Les Aspin concludes, "one discovers a huge Soviet defense manpower budget of over $50 billion that exists only in American documents."

The discovery of the spending gap fueled demands for regular increases in U.S. military spending measured in "real" dollars (over and above the inflation rate). In a time of government retrenchment, when efficiency and productivity have become watchwords of the society, defense had become the one public problem to be solved by throwing money at it. In any other policy matter—health, housing, transportation—a prescription to increase the federal budget indefinitely by 5 percent a year without demonstrating the specific need or utility of the items purchased would not be taken seriously. The defense budget is peculiarly susceptible to such a gross approach because neither generals nor legislators really know how much is enough. A dollar standard for judging the contestants in the arms race is easier than counting missiles or armies because the forces are difficult to compare. In judging the effectiveness of armies and missile forces, technological superiority is a critical and largely unmeasurable factor. Then, too, the U.S. and Soviet forces have different missions. According to the U.S. Defense Department's 1979 Annual Report, "at least 22 per cent of the increase in the Soviet defense budget during these 13 years (1964–1977) has been attributed to the buildup in the Far East." This reality renders gross comparison of U.S. and Soviet spending rates somewhat misleading. The Soviets have forty-four divisions on the Chinese frontier and thirty-one in Central Europe of which nine are stationed in Czechoslovakia and Hungary. The combined U.S.–NATO defense budgets are greater than the combined U.S.S.R.–Warsaw Pact expenditures, and if one sets aside the China-directed Soviet military expenditures, the spending gap in favor of the West is about twenty-five percent.

But defense spending is an index of intentions. That the Soviets are willing year after year to devote to the military establishment a considerably higher fraction of their considerably smaller national wealth suggests that they are determined to stay in the arms race and that they will never again willingly revert to a position of obvious military inferiority. Some American advocates of greatly increased military spending, including Ronald Reagan, argue that the Soviets are bent on gaining military superiority over the United States, but that if the U.S. resumes the spending race seriously the Kremlin will eventually give up because their smaller and weaker economy will not be able to stand the strain. The spending gap is a consequence of the relative weakness of their economy and the relative inefficiency of their military production. Being "outspent" by the Soviets ought to be seen more as a badge of their weakness than as a threat. Still, "there is no evidence to support the contention," as Secretary of Defense Harold Brown said upon leaving office, that the Soviets will abandon the arms race. The U.S. started the postwar era with a monopoly of nuclear weapons and the only economy left intact in the industrial world. The Soviets made their most significant postwar territorial gains when they were still reeling from the invasion that had cost them twenty million casualties, and they began to acquire a modern military machine while their economy was still in shambles. The Kremlin leaders seem prepared to sacrifice consumer goods and future industrial growth to keeping up in the military competition.

The rubles the Soviets spend hurt them more than they hurt the United States. Spending money does not necessarily translate itself into military power, much less political power. But a genuine "missile gap" is another matter. If the Soviets could neutralize the U.S. nuclear strike force, this could be translated into an enormous political advantage. The Soviet Union, according to Secretary of Defense Harold Brown, "within another year or two" will have "the necessary combination of ICBM reliability, numbers, warhead yields, and accuracies to put most of our Minuteman and Titan silos at risk."

The nuclear forces of the United States are designed to deter. Since they are meant to produce psychological rather than physical consequences—there is no national-security objective to be served once thousands of nuclear weapons have been detonated—almost as much attention has been lavished on advertising nuclear weapons as on designing them. As the arms race has accelerated, subtle changes in official language to describe the nuclear balance has occurred. In his statement on United States military posture for fiscal year 1975, Admiral Thomas H. Moorer, then Chairman of the Joint Chiefs of Staff, characterized the U.S.–Soviet strategic relationship as one of "dynamic equilibrium" or "relative strategic parity." Six years later in the FY 1981 statement on military posture his successor, General David C. Jones, concluded that "the strategic balance is shifting in favor of the Soviet Union, and the shift can only be halted by a serious commitment to extensive improvements in U.S. Forces." At about the same time Secretary of Defense Harold Brown reported, "By most relevant measures, we remain the military equal or superior to the Soviet Union."

How the military balance is described is more than a theological exercise for defense strategists. The words are chosen carefully with a view to their impact on three distinct audiences: the U.S. public and their representatives in Congress; allies and clients; and, of course, the Russians. To exact major increases in military spending it has been traditional, as Senator Arthur Vandenberg advised President Truman, to "scare hell out of the country." Nixon's first Secretary of Defense, Melvin Laird, tried to sell the antiballistic missile by announcing that "the Soviets are going for a first strike, there is no doubt about it." One billion dollars was wasted on a hopelessly impractical atomic-powered airplane on the strength of an erroneous intelligence report that the Soviets were building one. But the very statements designed to scare legislators into appropriating more money for weapons have the potential to mislead the Russians. Emphasizing U.S. weakness, as William E. Colby, former CIA director, points out, undermines the credibility of the U.S. nuclear deterrent. It also confuses allies who want U.S. military forces large enough to keep the Russians peaceful but not so large as to make them nervous. Since, as General Jones points out, "there is not a single military balance which must be evaluated, but rather several functional and cross-cutting balances, each of which portrays a different relative mix of strengths and weaknesses," the evaluation of relative strength depends upon where you start, what you count, and what you project.

Defense spending may be, Harold Brown argues, "the best single crude measure of relative military capabilities" because the Soviets are relatively less inefficient in military matters than in the civilian economy. But a serious assessment must look at what they have built, what they continue to build, and what specific new threats their weapons programs pose.

In the last decade the United States increased its stock of deployable nuclear warheads from 3,950 to 9,200, while the Soviet stockpile grew from 1,659 to 7,000. As Henry Kissinger once noted while in office, it is bombs and warheads rather than missiles that destroy targets. The Soviets have, however, far surpassed the United States in the deployment of new missiles. They have installed since 1969 three new models of intercontinental ballistic missiles and three new submarine-launched ballistic-missile systems. In the same period the United States deployed the Minuteman III, the Poseidon and a few Trident I submarine-launched missiles. The result is the much-publicized numbers gap. The Soviets now have 2,582 "delivery vehicles" (the standard euphemism for bombers and missiles), while the U.S., having eliminated more than 200 obsolete missiles, has only 2,048.

There are two levels at which this gap can be considered —one technical, the other strategic. As a technical matter there is much less of a gap than the numbers suggest because the new inertial guidance installed on 550 Minuteman IIIs has enormously increased their accuracy. Each warhead, according to calculations of D. C. Kephart of the Rand Corporation, is nearly three times more likely to destroy a hardened Soviet ICBM silo than the missile system it replaced. The Mk-12A warhead now being added to three hundred Minuteman IIIs doubles the explosive yield and further increases the probability of destroying hard targets. Whether these improvements increase or decrease U.S. security is itself a matter of debate and will be discussed below, but the impression that the United States has been standing still in the 1970s is erroneous. As Congressman Les Aspin summarizes the decade in the *Bulletin of the Atomic Scientists,* "The power of U.S. warheads has thus kept pace with the Soviet Union's, even with additional missiles." The cost is "several orders of magnitude cheaper than building a new missile." According to Aspin:

> The Soviets have spent tens of billions of dollars on new missiles, but we have continued to overwhelm them in deployment of new warheads; we have matched them in hard-target-kill capability with just a billion dollars' worth of new guidance systems and warheads; and we have degraded Soviet missile power by upgrading our missile silos at low cost.

The U.S. has also developed the air-launched cruise missile that can fly lower than one hundred feet from the ground and deliver within one hundred feet of a target warheads eleven times more powerful than the bomb that destroyed Hiroshima. President Carter's decision to cancel the B-1 bomber was not, as some critics have argued, an act of unilateral restraint. "The B-1, a very expensive weapons system, basically conceived in the absence of the cruise missile factor, is not necessary," the President declared. William Perry, the Pentagon's chief scientist, testified in 1979 that developments in Soviet air defense rendered the B-1 impractical. Because it is much smaller and can fly lower, the cruise missile is a much more threatening weapon—and much cheaper. To counter it, Dr. Perry suggests, would require the Soviets to spend $30 to $50 billion over the next decade.

Because of the obsolescence of the Polaris and Poseidon submarines, which are normally retired after twenty-five years, the number of U.S. submarine-launched missiles will be reduced from 656 to 384 by 1992. But a substantial portion of these missiles are being fitted with vastly more powerful and more accurate warheads (Trident I missiles carry eight 100-kiloton warheads replacing missiles bearing 40-kiloton warheads). The new Trident II will carry fourteen warheads. This means that each submarine commander will be able to land the equivalent of eleven Hiroshima bombs on 336 separate and dispersed targets.

Both superpowers have been proceeding inexorably with the nuclear arms race throughout the last decade, each in its own way. The question raised by the increasingly strident chorus of critics of the defense establishment who demand a quantum jump in military spending is whether Soviet weapons developments have given them new political capabilities.

The attainment of "strategic parity or even an overall advantage by the Soviet Union," according to the Chairman of the Joint Chiefs of Staff, General David C. Jones, does not mean that there is "a realistic possibility of a Soviet 'bolt-out-of-the-blue' strategic attack" on the United States. The strategic forces are sufficient "to absorb a Soviet first strike" and to "inflict major destruction on the Soviet Union." Over fifteen years ago the Department of Defense pointed out that if one hundred nuclear warheads landed on the Soviet Union, 37 million people, or 15 percent of the population, would die instantly and 59 percent of the industrial capacity would be destroyed. If three hundred such warheads were to land on target, 96 million people would die and 77 percent of the industrial capacity would be destroyed. The Soviet Union has five major population centers and 245 other cities with a population of 100,000 or more. Given these realities, a stockpile of five hundred deliverable nuclear weapons represents enormous "overkill." Even if the worst assumptions of U.S. military planners prove correct and the Soviets develop the capacity in the 1980s to destroy 90 percent of the U.S. land-based missiles, the submarines, cruise missiles and bombers would be able to deliver far more than 500 nuclear warheads on the Soviet Union.

But grisly arithmetic does not dispose of the issue, because nuclear weapons are designed to serve more varied and subtle purposes than deterrence of an all-out attack. In the 1950s and 1960s the U.S. had such clear "superiority" in nuclear weapons as to constitute what some defense planners call a "credible first-strike posture." The U.S. could launch a surprise attack on the Soviet Union and paralyze the Kremlin's ability to retaliate because the Soviet's relatively small stock of bombers and missiles could be targeted in advance by the much larger U.S. force. At the time of the Cuban Missile Crisis of October 1962, the Soviets had fewer than seventy missiles that could reach the U.S. In the era of "superiority," the U.S. officially subscribed to the view that its threat to initiate nuclear war was a crucial counterweight to Soviet "superiority" in ground forces. The Soviets had a mirror-image version of U.S. doctrine. At a time when the U.S. had a monopoly of nuclear weapons their only deterrent was to hold West Europe hostage. In Stalin's time their announced strategy in the event of a U.S. nuclear attack was to occupy all of Europe. Beginning in the late 1950s they began to target European cities with medium-range nuclear missiles.

In the era of "nuclear superiority" U.S. strategic doctrine called for "massive retaliation"—the use of nuclear weapons "at times and places of our own choosing," as John Foster Dulles put it, to deter or to punish "unacceptable" Soviet actions. On several occasions high U.S. officials considered using the atomic bomb. In 1952 Harry Truman mused about the possibility of eliminating Moscow, Leningrad (called St. Petersburg in his private notes that have recently been made public) and a ring of other cities if the Soviet Union did not settle quickly in Korea. A few months later his successor, Dwight D. Eisenhower, conveyed to the Chinese via the Indian government an explicit threat to use nuclear weapons, and in his memoirs he expresses his belief that his action ended the war. In the Kennedy Administration, Arthur Schlesinger, Jr., reports, the use of nuclear weapons was considered in the 1961 Berlin crisis.

Since the 1960s, however, first-strike strategies are no longer credible. The nuclear-arms race began in earnest only after the Cuban Missile Crisis. For the first postwar generation the United States was, as President Kennedy's Science Adviser, Jerome B. Wiesner, put it, "running the arms race with itself." Within the last ten years the Soviet Union has acquired enough of a strike force to deliver a devastating retaliatory attack on the U.S. A first-strike strategy is no longer possible for either side.

Nevertheless, new uses for nuclear weapons have been discovered which keep the arms race going. Presidential Directive 59 adopted in July 1980 calls for increasing U.S. capacity to fight a "prolonged but limited nuclear war." Since the McNamara era defense strategists have been pressing for more "counterforce capabilities"—that is, weapons designed to knock out weapons. In his annual report for fiscal year 1981 Harold Brown says that in addition to "second-strike forces necessary to attack a comprehensive set of targets" there should be additional forces held in reserve that could be used against "selected targets." Under the new presidential directive these will increasingly be military targets. There should be enough of a residual force to carry on a war "for a substantial period after a strategic exchange."

If the official function of the nuclear force is to target weapons and to keep hitting them months after a "strategic exchange," no set number of bombs or missiles is enough. Every weapon the Soviets build must be matched; every technological improvement in their defense—the achievement of greater accuracy or reduced vulnerability—must be offset. Once the nuclear force is regarded as a "flexible" instrument for achieving purposes beyond the crude one of deterring a nuclear attack with the threat of an all-out counterattack on Soviet society, the arms race becomes a never-ending, infinitely escalating contest.

The announcement a few days before the 1980 Democratic national convention that the United States had now officially embraced a "counterforce" strategy was the culmination of an eighteen-year planning effort. On June 16, 1962, Secretary of Defense Robert McNamara declared that the principal goal of U.S. strategy in a nuclear war "should be the destruction of the enemy's military forces, not his civilian population." In the 1960s U.S. strategic programs began to emphasize greater accuracy and power for the nuclear strike force. As the 1970s dawned, President Nixon called for a limited counterforce capability in his first foreign policy address to Congress:

> Should the President, in the event of a nuclear attack, be left with the single option of the ordering the mass destruction of enemy civilians in the face of the certainty that it would be followed by the mass slaughter of Americans? Should the concept of assured destruction be narrowly defined and should it be the only measure of our ability to deter the variety of threats we might face?

Four years later, on January 10, 1974, Secretary of Defense James Schlesinger announced "a new targeting doctrine that emphasizes selectivity and flexibility." Such public pronouncements are designed as signals to the Russians, as justifications for new weapons programs, and, perhaps most importantly, as a concession to disarm hawkish critics. The highly secret blueprint for conducting nuclear war is called

SIOP (single integrated operational plan). According to former high Pentagon officials, for more than twenty years it has included both military and nonmilitary targets.

The new public emphasis on weapons to hit weapons is a consequence of what William Colby calls the "paper and pencil war." U.S. military planners with computers constantly strive to increase their "options." In the paper and pencil war, the side with the better options wins. As Paul Nitze, former Pentagon official and leading advocate of increased military spending, puts it, "it is possible to think of highly plausible scenarios, assuming a position of Soviet superiority, and a deterioration of crisis stability, in which, should the balloon go up, the outcome would be highly one-sided."*

Under the Nitze theory the Soviets could "win" in a counterforce exchange once they were in a position to wreak greater destruction on the U.S. missile force than the U.S. could wreak on their own. In such a situation, the proponents of counterforce argue, the President of the United States, after a surprise Soviet attack on the vulnerable land-based missiles, would have no option but to launch an all-out war that would destroy both societies, or to surrender. But if the U.S. had an equivalent or superior counterforce capability, then the Kremlin version of the Pentagon computer model could not print out a first-strike option. The men in the Kremlin would proceed more cautiously and peace would be preserved.

The trappings of nuclear strategy are computers, mathematical models, and topographical curves. The entire purpose of the nuclear arsenal is to influence the behavior of six or seven Soviet leaders. As an education system, it has the highest per-pupil cost of any in the world. The argument between "doves" and "hawks" is only marginally an argument about relative technical capabilities; it is principally a

* Alan Tonelson, "Nitze's World," *Foreign Policy,* Fall 1979, pp. 78, 79.

disagreement about the psychology of Soviet leaders. If the United States is unable to undertake a "limited" retaliation against a Soviet attack, the United States will be "perceived" by Soviet leaders and third countries alike as weak, and over time the Soviets will score political victories.

Many experienced national-security specialists make a completely different assessment of Soviet psychology. Secretary of Defense Harold Brown, in his 1979 Annual Report, noted that it is not "at all clear that an initial use of nuclear weapons—however selectively they might be targeted—could be kept from escalating to a full-scale thermonuclear exchange, especially if command-control centers were brought under attack." Within the past five years both President Carter and Chairman Leonid Brezhnev have publicly stated that a limited nuclear war is implausible. For the losing side, indeed for any belligerent, the devastation caused by even a small nuclear attack would create nearly irresistible political and psychological pressures to escalate the war.

The advocates of moderation in military spending have a triple argument. First, they question whether a "counterforce gap" exists. There are so many imponderables in predicting the success of a disarming strike that no rational leader would try one. Even a "surgical" attack on the Minuteman silos could cause up to twenty-two million American deaths, according to former Secretary of Defense Harold Brown. As Leslie H. Gelb, former head of the Bureau of Politico-Military Affairs in the Department of State, pointed out in *Fortune,* "The Soviets would have to assume retaliation against their cities." Second, even if a theoretical gap existed, weapons stockpiles are now, unlike the time of the Cuban Missile Crisis, so high on both sides that the risks of escalation preclude using nuclear weapons as political instruments. (In that crisis, it should be recalled, the U.S. did not threaten to use nuclear weapons first, only to retaliate with nuclear weapons in the event the nuclear missiles in Cuba were fired.) Third, feverish preparations to counter nuclear war by design actually make nuclear war by miscalculation more likely.

The race to achieve counterforce capability makes military planners on both sides increasingly nervous. "We and the Soviet Union," Harold Brown told the graduating class at the U.S. Naval Academy in 1979, "are reaching a period in which each can successfully target the other's hardened fixed systems more cheaply than either can further harden its systems to make them survive." Weapons targeted on other weapons are presumptively "first-strike" weapons; empty silos from which missiles have already been launched are not worth spending billions to hit. Even if, as is probably the case, neither side has an intention to strike first, the military posture of the adversaries appears otherwise. What looks like a defensive countermove in Washington looks offensive in Moscow. As soon as Presidential Directive 59 on the shift to counterforce strategy was announced, a Soviet spokesman pronounced it "ominous," a judgment shared by American advocates of arms control who point out that the world is moving to a hair-trigger military environment in which the pressures to launch a "preemptive" strike to save the increasingly vulnerable missiles are mounting.

The more vulnerable the land-based missiles become, the greater the pressure to adopt a "launch-under-attack" strategy. "Very low survivability of ICBM's in the early 1980's will," according to the Department of Defense 1980 Posture Statement, "leave us with very little effective quick-response hard-target kill capability unless we were to adopt a launch-under-attack policy. . . ." The most consistent advocates of increased military spending see the dangers. As Paul Nitze told the House Armed Services Committee:

An important issue surrounding the launch-under-attack option is "launch what against what Soviet targets—upon what degree of evidence that an attack of what size is under way against U.S. targets?" Extremely difficult considerations are involved in answering that complex question. Should the President be asked to resolve them in the few minutes which may be available to him, or should the answers be preprogrammed into a computer? Neither alternative is without immense dangers.

As Fred C. Iklé, former head of the U.S. Arms Control and Disarmament Agency and a top Reagan defense adviser, noted in an interview in *Fortune,* a "launch-under-attack" system puts "incredible responsibilities on some tech sergeant in the innards of the system. The more quick and automatic it is, the more you're turning over decisions—the most fateful decision in the nation's history—to people far removed from the President and the Joint Chiefs."

On three recent occasions, one in the fall of 1979 and the others in the spring of 1980, military computers erroneously indicated that the Soviet Union had launched some of its nuclear missiles against the United States. On the first such occasion, a technician inadvertently ran a test tape through the computer system that triggered the commencement of the retaliatory process. In June 1980, a computer malfunction was blamed. Strategic bomber crews were ordered to their planes and the silo-based missiles were brought to a higher state of readiness after audio and visual signals showed that the Soviets had launched both submarine-based and land-based missiles. Within three minutes the alert was called off. Declaring that "we weren't remotely close to World War III," Assistant Secretary of Defense Thomas B. Ross declined to comment on the suggestion that a similar malfunction might trigger a series of escalating responses in the U.S. and the U.S.S.R. that could get out of hand. While Assistant Secretary Ross was reassuring Americans that the overanxious computer was being removed, David Jones, Chairman of the Joint Chiefs, was publicly suggesting that the Soviets take the incident as a warning. "They had better know that we are ready and that we can respond in a very few minutes."

The advocates of more missiles argue that the bigger and more survivable the U.S. force the less the pressure to adopt a "launch-under-attack" posture. But every gain in this direction helps raise the specter for the Soviets of a U.S. drive to achieve a "first-strike" posture. Such gain can be offset by a corresponding Soviet innovation. In a world in which both sides are rapidly "modernizing" their nuclear forces, military planners inevitably become more nervous and hair-trigger responses appear increasingly unavoidable. The advocates of arms control argue that in a calmer, less hostile, and more predictable military environment the risks of miscalculation are significantly reduced.

Discussions of the gap between Soviet perceptions of the arms race and U.S. perceptions have probably influenced thinking on defense in recent years more than the spending gap or the missile gap. Without the assumption that the U.S.–Soviet arms race is an asymmetrical contest, the projected U.S. arms buildup makes no sense. We are not hurt by the money the Russians spend. Nor do additions to Soviet overkill capacity cause us to be less secure. If the U.S. has enough deliverable nuclear warheads to cause "unacceptable" damage to the Soviet Union in a retaliatory attack —and the destructive power on one nuclear submarine would appear to be enough, given what one hundred weapons will do—what is the argument for building more?

Harold Brown argues that while a decision to rely on submarine-based missiles and cruise missiles "could be viewed as playing to U.S. strengths," a failure to modernize the ICBM force with a new mobile land-based missile system "would be to accept inferiority, or at least as evidence that we were not competitive in a major (indeed, what the Soviets have chosen as *the* major) area of strategic power." The perception of asymmetry would, according to defense analyst Barry Blechman, "make them a little gutsier and us a little more timid."

Such statements about the need to counter "perceptions" of military weakness even when no actual weakness exists have in the past two years become conventional wisdom. Curiously, Blechman is the co-author (with Stephen Kaplan) of *Force Without War: U.S. Armed Forces as a Political Instrument,* a Brookings Institution study of 215 incidents in which the U.S. used armed force as a political instrument from 1946 to 1975 which concluded:

> In general, the data do not support propositions as to the importance of the strategic balance. It was not true that positive outcomes were proportionately less frequent, the less the U.S. advantage vis-à-vis the Soviet Union in the number of either nuclear warheads or delivery vehicles. . . . We did not find that the United States was less often successful as the Soviet Union closed the U.S. lead in strategic nuclear weapons that had been maintained for the first twenty or so years following the Second World War.

Paul Warnke, former SALT negotiator, points out that perceptions of weakness are more likely to be stimulated by the irresponsible charges of retired generals and hawkish professors than by the failure to make marginal additions to the already enormous missile force. Modern Paul Reveres such as the Committee on the Present Danger, in their zeal to make the U.S. stronger in the future, emphasize present weakness. If the Soviets believed them, they might become more daring in resorting to "nuclear blackmail."

Presidential Directive 59, announcing a "war-fighting" strategy for the United States, was designed as an answer to the "war-fighting" strategy which has been imputed to the Soviets by defense critics in the last four years. The United

States, according to an array of former national-security officials who have campaigned through such organizations as the Committee on the Present Danger and the American Security Council, can no longer afford to rely on MAD (mutual assured destruction) as its principal strategy of war prevention. It is immoral, they say, since the U.S. is threatening to kill tens of millions of innocent Russians in retaliation for the provocative acts of their leaders over whom they have no control. Since the United States has refused to renounce the first use of nuclear weapons, a nuclear strike on population centers in the U.S.S.R. could well be ordered in retaliation for something less than a Soviet nuclear attack. But the principal point the critics of MAD make is that the Russians are playing a different game. Thus the whole expensive effort to create a properly cautious state of mind inside the Kremlin is misconceived. True deterrence requires matching the Russians at their own game.

The moral issue raised by the advocates of a U.S. "war-fighting" strategy is deceptive. It is presumably more "moral" to hit missiles rather than people, but in fact a counterforce strike involves hitting both missiles and people. To "take out" 150 Minuteman missiles at the Whiteman Air Force Base in Sedalia, Missouri, would require the Soviets to launch about three hundred of their missiles. According to NBC, based on information provided by the Pentagon, the "zone of total destruction" would exceed the size of the state of Delaware. If westerly winds prevailed, as is usually the case, fallout would reach St. Louis, where half the population would die. Louisville and Cincinnati would also lie in the track of the hypothetical "counterforce" attack. "Millions would be poisoned by radiation," the NBC report concludes.

Thus the argument against developing a "war-fighting" strategy is that such counterforce attacks with the huge casualties they cause would lead to more explicit countercity attacks. In other words, a "war-fighting strategy" is not a substitute for MAD, but a supplement. Far from being an alternative to the "suicide-or-surrender" dilemma, it offers an illusion of victory that makes nuclear war seem less unthinkable, and hence makes it more likely.

But the favorite argument for the adoption of a "war-fighting" strategy is that the Soviets have one. The Soviets, indeed, are developing a counterforce capability of their own —more accurate warheads, greater numbers of more powerful missiles that can knock out missiles. As in the case of every major technological development of the postwar arms race, they have started far behind the United States but have strived to imitate U.S. technological achievements—usually about five years after they have been deployed by the Americans. Thus, the first Soviet MIRV (multiple independently targeted reentry vehicle) test occurred in 1973, three years after the U.S. had deployed MIRVs.

According to Richard Pipes, a professor of Russian history at Harvard who has been a theoretician for the Committee on the Present Danger and a Reagan defense adviser, "the Soviet Union thinks it can fight and win a nuclear war." An examination of Soviet military journals convinces him that the Soviets believe they can accomplish political objectives by threatening and, if necessary, fighting a nuclear war. Because they have better civil defense they will suffer less damage and hence will win.

Contemporary Soviet military theorists share Lenin's famous enthusiasm for Clausewitz. In *Military Strategy*, the standard Soviet military text, the late Marshal V. D. Sokolovsky states that "the essential nature of war as a continuation of politics does not change with changing technology and armaments." For Pipes the repetition of the Clausewitzian maxim means that "mutual deterrence does not really exist." This extraordinary logical leap ignores much of what Soviet theorists say. In *Marxism-Leninism on War and Army*, written by a committee of leading Soviet officers and military analysts, the Clausewitzian point is spelled out:

Politics will determine when the armed struggle is to be started and what means are to be employed. Nuclear war cannot emerge from nowhere, out of a vacuum, by itself . . . war cannot be understood without first understanding its connection with the policies preceding it. . . . The political interests of the classes at war and of their conditions determine the war aims, while armed struggle is the means of achieving these aims . . . [W]ar is the continuation of the politics of definite classes and conditions by violent means.

It is precisely the fact that Soviet leaders do see war as an extension of politics that gives us hope of avoiding it. Soviet leaders are hardly pacifists, but they do not go to war without a good reason. There is, George Kennan points out, "no limited objective, no limited danger, no special fear, no ambition, no local situation" that could "conceivably justify" a nuclear war—for the Soviets no less than for ourselves.

General K. Bochkarev, deputy commandant of the General Staff Academy, writing in the military journal *Voyennaya Mysl'* (Military Thought) in 1968 calls nuclear war an "adventuristic gamble," but he goes on to note that "there is no serious proof that it has already been discarded by the general staffs of the Western powers, and above all by the Pentagon." In a passage that has been cited by American critics as evidence that the Soviets are planning a nuclear war, he criticizes the notion that there can be no winners in a nuclear contest. Such a belief would mean that "the very call to raise the combat readiness of our armed forces and improve their capability to defeat any aggressor is senseless." Morale rests on "the ideology of Marxism-Leninism which . . . instills in [our forces] unflagging confidence in the indestructibility and final triumph of the forces of socialism."

The Soviet military face the same problem as their American counterparts: the need year after year to maintain the readiness of forces that are designed not to be used and offer no hope of victory. To build an armed force on the prospect of either permanent inaction or annihilation is a virtually impossible task. This reality leads military planners on both sides to develop war-winning fantasies and to write for themselves documents which alarm their opposite numbers. U.S. military officers have written bloodcurdling scenarios about a successful first strike on the Soviet Union. In a review of Soviet military journals, Fred Kaplan, formerly defense-policy adviser to U.S. Representative Les Aspin, finds their message to be "that the Soviets will *not* use nuclear weapons for political gain, but that they suspect the United States might and that therefore the Soviet camp must be prepared to make the best of things if war does erupt." * At the highest political level the Soviets have grasped the meaning of nuclear war. "The starting of a nuclear missile war," Leonid Brezhnev declared at the thirtieth-anniversary celebration of the World War II victory, "would spell inevitable annihilation for the aggressor himself, to say nothing of the vast losses for many other countries perhaps not even formally involved in the war."

Yet the Soviet civil-defense program is offered as evidence that the Soviets are following a strategy other than mutual assured destruction. Their plans for evacuation and protection of industry, according to some critics, mean that the Soviets could suffer "only 5 to 25 million casualties—they suffered 20 million in World War II—and recover. According to retired General Daniel O. Graham, former director of the Defense Intelligence Agency, testifying before the Senate Foreign Relations Committee:

> The Soviets evacuate their cities and hunker down. Then they move against NATO or Yugoslavia or China or the Middle East with superior conventional forces.

* Fred Kaplan, *Dubious Specter: A Skeptical Look at the Soviet Nuclear Threat* (Washington, D.C.: The Institute for Policy Studies, 1980).

The United States is faced with the demand to stay out or risk nuclear exchange in which 100 million Americans would die, as opposed to 10 million Russians.

The Central Intelligence Agency has a different view of Soviet civil defense. The Soviets, it points out, have never conducted an evacuation drill in a major city or entirely emptied even a small town. CIA Director Stansfield Turner found "little evidence today of serious efforts at mass indoctrination of the population" on civil defense. The CIA also concludes that there is "little evidence . . . that would suggest a comprehensive program for hardening economic installations. . . . Overall, the measures the Soviets have taken to protect their economy would not prevent massive damage from an attack designed to destroy Soviet economic facilities." A study by the U.S. Office of Technology Assessment concludes that three Minuteman III ICBMs and seven Poseidon missiles with multiple warheads could wipe out 73 percent of the Soviet industrial refining capacity; indeed, according to another official study, 75 percent of the basic industrial capacity—primary metals, chemicals, petroleum construction, agricultural and railroad equipment, synthetic rubber and power generators—is concentrated in four hundred plants. Since one Trident submarine could destroy more than three hundred cities, and even the attempt at mass evacuation would run great risks of triggering a U.S. response, the Soviets have no way of converting their continuing low-level civilian-defense efforts into a successful "war-winning strategy."

While most of the ominous interpretations of the "present danger" posed by Soviet expansionism fasten on the nuclear balance, the Committee on the Present Danger, Ronald Reagan, and other critics also express concern about the nonnuclear military balance. The Soviet Union has a bigger army than the United States, but the United States and NATO have 5.1 million men under arms while the Soviets, even including one million Warsaw Pact troops of doubtful reliability, have 4.8 million. In his 1981 Annual Report, Defense Secretary Brown concludes that in Central Europe "a rough numerical balance exists between the immediately available non-nuclear forces of NATO (including France) and those of the Warsaw Pact." The Soviets and their East European allies outnumber the West in tanks three to one, but NATO far outnumbers the Warsaw Pact in antitank weapons. Since the purpose of NATO is defensive, it makes sense to invest in technology to stop tanks rather than to engage in a tank-collecting contest.

Until the détente era no one talked about a U.S.–Soviet naval arms race. The U.S. Navy was supreme. There was virtually no bit of water in the world beyond the reach of a U.S. armada. The Soviet Union was largely landlocked; most of its ports were frozen much of the year. Czarist Russia had never been a sea power. It was highly improbable that Soviet Russia would become one. Within the last five years, however, the mood has shifted dramatically. There is no question that there has been a Soviet naval buildup. The controversial issues have to do with its extent and significance. As in the nuclear-arms race, numbers can be used to create wildly different pictures of the world. Advocates of a bigger U.S. Navy note that the Soviets have more ships today than the United States. But this is misleading, since most of them are small and designed for coastal defense. The U.S. Navy is made up of far larger and more powerful ships and, unlike the Soviet Navy, is able to project its power on a global scale.

But the Soviet Union is adding to its naval power at the rate of about ten surface ships a year. At the end of World War II the Soviet Navy was a coastal defense force—in effect, a branch of the Army. Gradually, in the fifties, the Soviets built nuclear submarines and ships to oppose U.S. carriers. They "show the flag" with port visits in the Third World with increasing frequency. Soviet naval forces were more visible in the eastern Mediterranean in the 1973 Arab–Israeli War than in the one six years earlier. Soviet naval units have been dispatched to aid clients in Africa on at least four occasions.

Although the Soviets have in recent years been building the Kiev-class aircraft carrier, guided-missile aviation cruisers, and other surface ships designed to project power at a distance or to attack U.S. ocean supply lines to Europe and Japan, they have virtually no capacity to land an expeditionary force by sea. (They do have seven airborne divisions. When these were alerted during the 1973 Middle East War, President Nixon ordered a worldwide alert of the U.S. nuclear forces.)

The U.S. naval forces are now sufficient, according to former Secretary of Defense Brown, in the event of a major war in Europe to bottle up the Soviet fleet in home waters and to eliminate substantially any Soviet naval contribution to the war. At the same time, growing Soviet submarine capability would take "as long as three months to control" during which "a significant percentage of U.S. and allied reinforcement and supply shipping" might be lost.

In the nuclear-arms race, whether there is "enough" depends upon the assumptions one makes about the uses of nuclear weapons. When Jimmy Carter came into office he asked the Pentagon to study the feasibility of reducing the strategic missile force from 1,800 to 200; three and a half years later he ordered substantial increases in the force. The rate of Soviet weapons acquisition had not substantially changed. American weapons theory had changed.

In nonnuclear forces, the debate about gaps and balances is equally unreal. Once the purpose of military spending is to create "perception," and weapons are procured primarily as symbols, there is never enough. Once enticed into the hermetic world of war games, statesmen lose touch with reality. Whether there is "enough" in fact depends upon what a future war will be like. If the past two world wars are any guide, it will bear little resemblance to the wars in the war plans. George Kennan, a leading exponent of the "realist" school in international relations, one who takes power seriously, sees the dangerous consequences of reducing national security to military gamesmanship:

> . . . this entire science of long-range massive destruction, of calculated advantage or disadvantage in modern weaponry has gotten seriously out of hand. The variables, complexities and uncertainties it involves have grown beyond the power of either human mind or computer.
>   . . . there is a distinct unreality about this whole science of destruction as the locus—the theater—in which our differences over policy have to be resolved. We are not going to solve our problems by trying to agree over whether the Russians will or will not have the capability of "taking out" our land-based missiles some time in the 1980's. This is not the heart of the problem; something deeper is involved.*

The arms race can neither be stopped nor be stabilized without a theory as to what lethal force, nuclear and nonnuclear, can do for a great nation in the nuclear age. That is a debate the nation has not yet had.

* George F. Kennan, "U.S.–Soviet Relations: Toward a New Approach to the USSR," *Current* July/August 1978, p. 39.

CHAPTER 3

The Carter Surrender

Instead a different debate has taken place over the last four years. The two questions that have come to dominate all discussions of national security are these: Is the United States becoming number two in military might? Is the Soviet Union bent on world domination?

The Carter Administration came into office with a quite different approach to national security. In his campaign the former Georgia governor criticized the Kissinger détente for being a "one-way street," but called for extending it. "We must replace balance-of-power politics with world order politics," he said in a *New York Times* interview in June 1976. "It is likely in the near future that issues of war and peace will be more a function of economic and social problems than of the military-security problems which have dominated international relations since World War II." The candidate promised a five- to seven-billion-dollar cut in the military budget. In his inaugural address he declared, "We will move this year toward our ultimate goal—the elimination of all nuclear weapons from this earth."

Although the notion of détente with the Russians had been saddled with so many negative connotations by its critics that the Ford Administration jettisoned the term before the

1976 campaign, there appeared to be a national consensus on arms control. In his final press conference, held ten days before Carter's inaugural, outgoing Secretary of State Henry Kissinger attacked the enemies of the SALT II treaty: "I do not believe the Soviet Union is achieving military superiority over the United States." Besides, he added, the whole idea of military superiority when each side can annihilate the other "has no operational significance. . . ." Those who are still talking about superiority "are not doing this country a service."*

More than two years before, Kissinger had taken on the enemies of détente in private. In the summer of 1974, a group called the Coalition for a Democratic Majority released a report of a task force chaired by Eugene Rostow, former Undersecretary of State, who believed that the U.S. had gone soft in Vietnam. "The Quest for Détente" was a wholesale attack on the Kissinger policy. The Russians could not be trusted. Nixon had claimed too much for détente Rostow told Kissinger in a personal letter: "And we think it is not only wrong, but dangerous to lull Western public opinion by proclaiming an end of the Cold War, a substitution for confrontation and a generation of peace." Kissinger had written Rostow two weeks earlier explaining his concept of U.S.–Soviet relations: "We have sought to rely on a balance of mutual interest rather than on Soviet intentions as expressed by ideological dogma. In dealing with the Soviets, we have, in a sense, appealed to the spirit of Pavlov rather than Hegel." But, like much of the parallel monologue that passes for debate on national security, the issues were never joined in the correspondence.

The foreign-policy establishment has always been divided over how to deal with the Soviet Union—this division reflects two radically different conceptions of what the Soviet

* "Kissinger says Idea of Supremacy Makes No Sense in a Nuclear Age," *The New York Times,* January 11, 1977.

Union is, each of which leads to virtually opposite strategies for taming the adversary. The first is the view that has prevailed for most of the period since 1950. It was articulated in NSC-68, "The Report by the Secretaries of State and Defense on 'United States Objectives and Programs for National Security,' " April, 7, 1950:

> . . . the Soviet Union, unlike previous aspirants to hegemony, is animated by a new fanatic faith, antithetical to our own, and seeks to impose its absolute authority over the rest of the world. Conflict has, therefore, become endemic . . .

The strategy for opposing Soviet ambitions was containment:

> As for the policy of "containment," it is one which seeks by all means short of war to 1) block further expansion of Soviet power, 2) expose the falsities of Soviet pretensions, 3) induce a retraction of the Kremlin's control and influence and 4) in general, so foster the seeds of destruction within the Soviet system that the Kremlin is brought at least to the point of modifying its behavior to conform to generally accepted international standards.

NSC-68 called for taking "dynamic steps to reduce the power and influence of the Kremlin inside the Soviet Union and other areas under its control," a policy that a few years later in the John Foster Dulles era would be termed "rollback" instead of "containment." The strategy was to include "operations by covert means in the fields of economic warfare and political and psychological warfare. In other words, it would be the current Soviet cold war technique used against the Soviet Union." It is "cardinal" to the policy that "we possess superior overall power."

> Without superior aggregate military strength, in being
> and readily mobilizable, a policy of "containment"—
> which is in effect a policy of calculated and gradual
> coercion—is no more than a policy of bluff.

Because the Soviet Union possesses armed forces "far in excess of those to defend its national territory," NSC-68 reached the conclusion that the U.S.S.R. "is developing the military capacity to support its design for world domination."

The other view of the Soviet Union was expressed during the deliberations on NSC-68 by the two senior Soviet specialists in the government, George Kennan and Charles E. Bohlen. The Soviet threat, Kennan argued, was primarily a political, economic, and diplomatic challenge. Kennan had had a profoundly alarming effect on the whole government in 1946 by sending from Moscow, where he was serving as counselor of the embassy, a long telegram which was designed to alert naive politicians in Washington, as he considered them, to the true nature of the Stalinist regime. He later reworked the telegram into an article, "The Sources of Soviet Conduct," which appeared in *Foreign Affairs* in 1947, signed only "Mr. X." In it he advised "the containment of Russian expansive tendencies . . . by the adroit and vigilant application of counterforce at a series of constantly shifting geographical points . . ." The analysis dovetailed with strategic thinking that was taking shape in Washington, and it became instantly influential. Twenty years later in his *Memoirs* he regretted his failure not to make clear "that what I was talking about when I mentioned the containment of Soviet power was not the containment by military means of a military threat, but the political containment of a political threat."

Thus the view of the Russians that competed with the apocalyptical message of NSC-68 also started by assuming that the men in the Kremlin were tough, cynical, and opportunistic. No doubt they wished the United States no good and, perhaps, they harbored dreams of world domination, but they were cautious pragmatists with enormous problems who wanted to make concrete deals with the West in areas where mutual interests dictated. W. Averell Harriman, like Kennan and Bohlen a former ambassador to Moscow who has known every Soviet leader since Lenin, has been an influential exponent of this view. (Ironically, like Kennan, he also was an early and vocal alarmist in the immediate postwar period.) In a 1974 conference on Capitol Hill he criticized Secretary of Defense James Schlesinger's hard-line statements:

> Tough statements by our Secretary of Defense or others have the same effect in Moscow as tough statements by Soviet Defense Minister Grechko have on us here. They pull the rug out from under the more moderate and strengthen the arguments of the militants and other hard-liners.

What divided the Kennans and the Harrimans from the Schlesingers and the Rostows was the assumption of the first group that American and Russian leaders exhibit the same human reactions to developments in the arms race. According to the NSC-68 view, the Russians despise compromise and "understand only force." They will make no concessions nor moderate their limitless appetite unless compelled to do it under military pressure. Any effort at accommodation will be regarded as evidence of weakness and will be cynically exploited. Kennan regards the view that the Soviet leaders operate by a totally different set of psychological and moral principles as an example of "a peculiarly American tendency to what I would call the dehumanization of any major national opponent: the tendency, that is, to form a species of devil-image of that opponent, to deprive him in our imaginations of all normal human attributes, and to see him as totally evil and devoted to nothing but our destruction.''

Until the Tet Offensive of February 1968, such critics of "overmilitarization" of American foreign policy were few. The request that month by the Joint Chiefs of Staff for 206,000 additional troops for Vietnam sparked an internal debate which soon led to a major split in the foreign-policy consensus. Clark Clifford, the new Secretary of Defense, the author of an early Truman administration memorandum that foreshadowed NSC-68, and known for his hard-line views, turned around dramatically. He began to accept the views of Paul Warnke, who worked for him as Assistant Secretary of Defense for International Security Affairs, that "we can keep on winning the war forever . . . and it won't ever make any difference . . . because there is no way we can bring about political progress in South Vietnam." * In short, there were limits to the political use of force. This was an idea that explicitly challenged the underpinnings of bipartisan wisdom, that it was possible, as Henry Kissinger once put it, "to create a military capability which can redress the balance in limited wars and which can translate our technological advantage into local superiority." Paul Nitze, who also worked for Clifford, emphasized the folly of an open-ended commitment in Southeast Asia which would sap forces needed elsewhere. But he did not accept the other challenge to the consensus which Warnke pressed:

What happens in Southeast Asia is of only marginal importance to the Soviet Union. Whether Hanoi wins or

* Quoted by John B. Henry in "February, 1968," *Foreign Policy* 4 (1971), p. 29

Saigon manages to hold on indefinitely is not going to
have the least impact on Russians in Egypt or Egyptians
in Russia or pressure on Berlin or anything else.

The different lessons Nitze and Warnke drew from the Vietnam experience would turn the two men into bitter antagonists.

The consensus cracked still further when the "wise men"
called in by Lyndon Johnson for outside advice, including
Dean Acheson, John J. McCloy, and other representatives
of the New York financial world, told the President that the
war was ruining the economy, imperiling relations with Europe, and losing the support of the country. Acheson, the
quintessential hard-liner, told the President over lunch that
"he was being led down a garden path by the JCS." For
seven years thereafter two administrations pursued a tor-
tuous path of disengagement from Indochina, a wrenching
process with the shocking denouement of an American ambassador being lifted by helicopter from the roof of the U.S.
Embassy just as Saigon was about to fall. During the long
process of "Vietnamization," Nixon and Kissinger tried to
hold on to the foreign-policy consensus by postponing the
defeat in Indochina and by accepting as a "lesson of Vietnam" the necessity of limiting American commitments.
American policy was as anti-Communist as ever. The as-
cendance of the Left, whether by election as in Chile or by
revolution as in Portugal, would be firmly resisted under the
traditional view that every regime of the Marxist left anywhere in the world was a gain for Russia and a defeat for the
United States. But the U.S. would no longer send in its own
troops. The draft would be ended; teenagers from the middle
class would not again be asked to cast an existential vote on
foreign military operations. Under the Nixon Doctrine,
friendly "regional powers" such as Iran, Zaire, and Brazil
would become surrogate peacekeepers. The burden would

no longer, as John F. Kennedy had put it, rest entirely on American shoulders.

A comprehensive debate on the world view that led the United States into the Vietnam "quagmire," as everyone came to call it, never took place. Although the Indochina defeat will most likely come to be seen as an historic turning point, at least as significant as Franklin Roosevelt's decision to end American isolationism by aiding Britain in 1940 or Harry Truman's decision to station permanent American forces in Europe, there was no comparable "Great Debate" in the 1970s. Instead, different constituencies chipped away at different aspects of the battered consensus. Important parts of the financial community blamed high military spending for the deterioration of the dollar, the gold outflow, and the inflation that began with the Vietnam War budgets. Military spending may have stimulated the economy in the past, but, a United Nations Association panel that included a number of bankers and corporate executives concluded, continued high levels of military spending were now stifling economic growth. In 1969, according to Gallup polls, 52 percent of the public thought too much money was being spent on defense. (In the years 1968–73 opposition to military spending remained at about 50 percent. In the pre-Vietnam period it was never more than 20 percent.)

In 1971 a group of professors and former junior Foreign Service officers, including Zbigniew Brzezinski, Samuel Huntington, Richard Holbrooke, and others who would assume important positions in the Carter Administration six years later, announced the publication of a new journal, *Foreign Policy*. The premise of the new magazine was that "an era in American foreign policy which began in the late 1940's, has ended." The contributions stressed "world order," "interdependence," and "global concern." The editors explained that "in the light of Vietnam, the basic purposes of American foreign policy demand re-examination and redefinition.'' In 1973 David Rockefeller organized the Trilateral Commission, a collection of bankers, industrialists, a few influential professors, and other prominent figures from the U.S., West Europe, and Japan to develop a new set of principles and proposals for the post-Vietnam world. The major premise was that the growing conflicts within the industrial world, the collapse of the Bretton Woods monetary arrangements, and the world energy crisis constituted the most urgent national-security problems. International relations should no longer be viewed through the prism of U.S.–Soviet confrontation. The Cold War was over. Zbigniew Brzezinski became the executive director of the group. Walter Mondale, Cyrus Vance, Paul Warnke, Harold Brown, and other future cabinet officers of the Carter Administration were invited to join. At the urging of the editor of *Time*, Hedley Donovan, former Georgia Governor James E. Carter, Jr., was added to the list.

The Trilateral Commission implicitly attacked the old Cold War consensus in a number of ways. The energy crisis of 1973 made it clear that the Soviet Union was not the source of all crises; there were many problems for which containment and anti-Communism were no answers at all. Relations between the Western industrial countries and the Third World had to be improved in the interests of protecting access to scarce resources and of rebuilding the world economy. Neither could be done by viewing political and economic change in the Third World as an arena of superpower confrontation. U.S.–Soviet tensions would, as Nixon's deteriorating relations with Europe made clear, split the industrial world at a time when cooperation among the developed countries was crucial to the national interest. Prosperity required the expansion of trade, and that in turn required reducing tensions between the United States and the Soviet Union. Prominent business leaders became spokesmen for détente. Donald Kendall, president of Pepsico and a friend of President Nixon, became a founder of the Committee for East–West Accord, a lobby for better relations with Russia that included executives from El Paso Natural Gas, Control Data Corporation, Brown Brothers Harriman, and other corporate and banking interests. Thornton Bradshaw, president of Arco, chaired a United Nations Association panel that called for a moratorium on U.S. and Soviet military spending.

In 1975, Paul Warnke in *Foreign Policy* wrote the most explicit challenge to the fundamental assumptions of national-security policy by anyone who had ever had a high position in the Pentagon. It was a "fiction that protection of our interests implies a global military mission" or that "a failure by the United States to maintain a cosmetic military 'superiority' will cause us political disadvantage . . . our preoccupation with military power as a political tool needs to be faced and overcome." The huge nuclear-weapons stockpiles, far in excess of what is needed to destroy the society of the other side, "serve only as offsets, not as exploitable resources." Hence "they are not translatable into sound political currency." Conventional military forces also have limited political effectiveness. The United States can neither control political and economic change in the former colonial world nor act as a global policeman.

The high-water mark of détente was 1974—the year of Nixon's visit to Moscow and the Vladivostok accords on nuclear weapons. The move back to the assumptions and policies of the Cold War began almost at the moment Richard Nixon was driven from office. (For many years the official Soviet explanation of Watergate was that the crisis had been invented by reactionary forces to get rid of the architect of détente.) By the fall of 1974, public-opinion polls registered a shift in the public mood. The number of Americans who wanted increased military spending almost doubled. In 1972 only 39 percent of the respondents to a Potomac Associates poll thought "the United States should maintain its dominant position as the world's most powerful nation at all costs, even going to the brink of war if necessary"; by May 1976, in the midst of the presidential primary campaign, 52 percent supported the statement. NBC surveys reported that voters in the early primary states by a wide margin believed that the Soviet Union had benefited more from détente than had the United States. The public-opinion analysts William Watts and Lloyd Free concluded that "there is a new desire to put an end to what is seen as weakening of the U.S. role in the world, and to resume the position of being 'number one.' "

In the summer of 1974, the Coalition for a Democratic Majority, a group of Democrats who had broken with George McGovern two years earlier over foreign policy, issued a task force report, "The Quest for Détente," an attack on the very idea that there could be an end to the Cold War. As Eugene Rostow, the author of the report, wrote Kissinger, "Soviet policy never changes." In June, Paul Nitze, who had served in one important national-security post or another in every administration since Truman's, resigned as a member of the delegation that was negotiating the SALT II treaty and told the Senate Armed Services Committee that the Administration was selling a "myth of détente." Nitze, Rostow, James Schlesinger, Nixon's hard-line Secretary of Defense, Charles Walker, former Deputy Secretary of the Treasury in the Nixon Administration, David Packard, a computer magnate who had also held a high post in the Defense Department, and Henry Fowler, Johnson's Secretary of the Treasury, continued to meet regularly through the first year of the Ford administration to discuss forming an influential group to attack détente, highlight the Soviet threat, and push for significant increases in military spending. In March 1976, over a lunch at the Metropolitan Club in Washington, the Committee on the Present Danger was organized.

In choosing the name, the organizers reached back to 1950 when James Bryant Conant, president of Harvard, Will Clayton, Robert Lovett and other former national-security officials founded an organization with the identical purpose. The inspiration for the original Committee on the Present Danger was Conant's: " 'Get a group of distinguished citizens together,' I said, 'draw up a program, put it before the public, get people to write Congress and . . . respond to the gravity of the situation. From what I have just heard, I judge the country is asleep. You should wake it up.' " * The committee was intended as a vast public relations effort for rearmament, universal military service, the stationing of troops in Europe, and the education of the public for a permanent Cold War. At its opening press conference on December 12, 1950, in the midst of a Chinese drive on MacArthur's forces in Korea, the committee declared that "the aggressive designs of the Soviet Union are unmistakably plain." (For Dean Rusk, then Assistant Secretary of State, as for many observers of the day, the Chinese were simply Russian "puppets.") The first Committee on the Present Danger achieved its goal brilliantly. When it disbanded three years later, military spending had tripled. The country had accepted the Cold War consensus. The assumptions of NSC-68 had become a part of the national consciousness.

In his study *Peddlers of Crisis*, comparing the two committees with the identical name separated by a quarter century, Jerry W. Sanders notes that some of the same people were identified with both efforts. Paul Nitze, who became the leading spokesman for the 1976 committee, worked informally with the earlier committee as a member of the State Department. Charles Tyroler, director of the 1976 committee, also had experience with the earlier one as a young Pentagon official. The issues, the language, and the tech-

* James B. Conant, *My Several Lives* (New York: Harper and Row, 1970), p. 509.

niques employed by the two groups were the same. Yet there were two important differences.

In 1950, as Professor Sanders notes, the organizers of the committee saw their role as support of the government. It could be effective, Conant wrote, "only if it were welcomed (unofficially, but sincerely) by the administration." On October 24, 1950, the organizers wrote Secretary of Defense George C. Marshall:

> Specifically, we have thought that one way in which such a committee might be of help would be in strengthening the public support for such stern measures as may be necessary. We of course do not wish to involve you in any way whatever relative to this proposal, and write this letter only because we would not wish to proceed if you felt it would not be constructive to do so.

Marshall wrote a personal note to each signatory of the letter —"Your proposal is an undertaking of great importance"— and invited the group for a private meeting. Consultant status and classified briefings were provided for committee members. In December 1952, the Committee met with President-elect Dwight D. Eisenhower. Conant, the chairman, and Tracy Voorhees, the vice-chairman, entered the new Administration, and the committee, now fully integrated into the government, shortly thereafter disbanded.

The 1976 Committee on the Present Danger was organized in opposition to Ford and Kissinger. In May 1976 Eugene Rostow wrote James Schlesinger, who had been dismissed as Secretary of Defense by President Ford for his anti-détente views:

> . . . I enclose a newspaper clipping about the President's recent speech before the American Jewish Committee. I believe the speech must be answered soon, and

strongly, in the election debate. I am urging some of the Democrats to speak out on the subject. If you agree, you might pass the enclosed package on to Governor Reagan, perhaps with your own outline of a possible speech.

The opposition to Carter ran deeper. Taking the Nitze position, the committee condemned the new Administration's SALT policy. In direct opposition to the "world order" rhetoric of the new Administration, the committee's opening statement declared that "the principal threat to our nation, to world peace, and to the cause of human freedom is the Soviet drive for dominance based upon an unprecedented military buildup." The new Administration included not a single member of the new committee, and when, in August 1977, a few of its leaders met with the President, the atmosphere was tense. According to the version given the columnists Evans and Novak by the committee members, Nitze was "dismayed" to hear the President argue that public opinion would not support a larger military budget. On the contrary, the President's visitor argued, the public was "ahead" of the leaders on the issue. Eugene Rostow had argued before the Democratic Platform Committee the year before that "a strong and angry tide of concern about the safety of the nation is running throughout the country." From the start, individual members of the committee attacked the national-security advisers of the new Administration, the pro-détente businessmen, and the "world order" intellectuals in harsh personal terms. The "isolationism" and "the culture of appeasement" of post-Vietnam America, as Norman Podhoretz called it in his book *The Present Danger,* was a sickness of an elite that had lost the "will" to proclaim the superiority of American values. The businessmen who supported better relations were, as Richard V. Allen, Ronald Reagan's national-security adviser put it in an interview with Sanders, "supercharged from vodka parties and the promise of hundreds of millions of orders." The naiveté "typical of commercial societies" kept the country, Richard Pipes asserted in *Commentary,* from paying "serious attention to military strategy." American intellectuals, afflicted with an unexplained "self-hatred," have since Vietnam "come to believe that the exercise of American power is immoral." The Carter Administration had lent authority to a new foreign-policy establishment that believed in transcending the Cold War. Once more, just as John F. Kennedy had proclaimed at his inauguration, the torch was passing. The self-appointed task of the Committee on the Present Danger was to get it back.

The second difference between the new committee and its predecessor of the same name was its political flavor. The first committee was bipartisan, but its Republicans were exclusively from the "internationalist" Eisenhower wing of the party. Fiscal conservatives, including members of the National Association of Manufacturers, opposed the big military budgets urged by the committee, on the grounds that the country couldn't afford it. Stalin's secret plan, the conservatives argued, was to bankrupt the Treasury. Moreover, the right wing of the Republican Party, led by Senator Robert A. Taft of Ohio, opposed sending troops to Europe, the building up of NATO, and other crucial aspects of the emerging internationalist consensus. Isolationists before the war, they now favored a military buildup, but only to fight what former President Herbert Hoover termed "the hordes of Asia," not "a hopeless land war with Russia and the massacre of American boys." These were the McCarthy years, and the committee members, spokesmen for Dean Acheson and General George Marshall, the hated targets of the right, became the targets of such attacks themselves.

In 1976, Sanders's research makes clear, it was quite different. The committee worked from its inception with right-wing groups and individuals that would have been highly suspicious of its predecessor. Frank Barnett, founder of the National Strategy Information Center, a pro-military lobby, was, as he himself put it, "by origin a Robert Taft Republican from Peoria, Illinois." In May 1976 he wrote Eugene Rostow that his organization had been given $1 million "to crank up an all-out effort to meet the current and growing threat from the USSR." He was moving to the nation's capital to set up "a full-scale Washington office" that would:

1) Interact with policy echelons in the White House and Pentagon (where we still have friends);
2) "Tutor" Congressional staffs and brief members;
3) Work with Trade Associations—with an interest in "defense"—which have Washington offices;
4) Generate more public information through friends in the Washington press corps who write about military and foreign affairs.

He invited Rostow to join his board. In accepting, the former Undersecretary of State noted that "our new Committee on the Present Danger, of which you will be an active member, is planning a comparable operation. It should be no problem to coordinate our activities and indeed to act jointly on many issues."

Within four years the committee had fought three major battles with the pro-détente forces in two administrations and, in the process, had helped to change dramatically American perceptions of the Russians and of themselves. The first battle began within weeks of the founding meeting of the committee. Under attack from Ronald Reagan in the Republican primaries, President Ford approved the appointment of outside experts to go over the CIA's intelligence data on the Soviet Union. The group of seven military and academic specialists selected for their "more somber views" of the Soviet threat quickly became known as Team B. The President's Foreign Intelligence Advisory Board, a sixteen-member body of which six were original members of the Committee on the Present Danger, had recommended such an outside evaluation a year earlier. The National Intelligence Estimates had been under attack for being overly complacent about the Russians. In a study of previous projections of Soviet strategic capabilities, Professor Albert Wohlstetter of the University of Chicago had concluded that forty-nine out of fifty-one had turned out to be underestimates. (There were, however, some highly influential overestimates, including Paul Nitze's erroneous projection of a coming "bomber gap" in 1954, which four years earlier he labeled the "year of maximum danger," and the Air Force's alarmist projection of Soviet missile production which was the basis of John F. Kennedy's equally misleading "missile gap" rhetoric in the 1960 campaign. In both cases the gaps existed, but they were heavily in favor of the U.S.)

"The composition of the B Team dealing with Soviet objectives was so structured," a 1978 report of the Senate Select Committee on Intelligence concluded, "that the outcome of the exercise was predetermined. . . . The intelligence agencies were cast inaccurately in the role of 'doves.' " ("There are more liberals per square foot in the CIA than in any other part of the government," General Daniel O. Graham, a member of Team B, told Sanders in August 1977.) Richard Pipes, the chairman of the group, denied being "hard-line," only "Clausewitsian . . . which is the way the Soviets look at it." *

The Team B report was never published, but its contents were leaked. Every element in the Committee on the Present Danger's analysis of the Soviet threat was included. The Soviets had a war-winning strategy, a dangerous civil-

* Murray Marder, "Carter to Inherit Intense Dispute on Soviet Intentions," *The Washington Post,* January 2, 1977.

defense program, and a plan to use "military superiority" over the United States to achieve their global designs. In a press conference, Major General George Keegan, the retiring chief of Air Force Intelligence, declared that the Soviets had already achieved superiority. "I am unaware of a single important category in which the Soviets have not established a significant lead over the United States." William Van Cleave, another member of Team B, endorsed the view, saying he would heartily favor trading defense establishments with the Soviets. The findings of Team B challenged years of work within the intelligence community. "It was an absolute disaster for the Agency," a CIA official told *The New York Times* in late December. According to a *Washington Post* report on January 2, 1977, "numerous sources on all sides agree that the 'peer pressures' on the insiders were great. Daniel Graham was reported to have said to the CIA group at one point: 'I don't want to tell you guys you're going to lose your jobs if you don't get on board, but that's the way it is.' " The *Post* account predicted that the Team B exercise, flawed as it was, would be influential: ". . . the encouragement given to pessimists or 'worst case' theorists on Soviet intentions inside the government, is regarded as a high barrier for the Carter Administration to overcome to carry out its broader objectives for U.S.–Soviet nuclear arms control." The notion that the Soviets "intend to surpass the United States in strategic arms and are in the process of doing so," in Senator Daniel P. Moynihan's words, had "gone from heresy to respectability, if not orthodoxy."

While the incoming Carter Administration was free to write its own intelligence estimates, the "somber views" of Team B had already dominated the debate. No new data had been discovered. There was no more than the usual disagreement within the intelligence community about numbers. The debate on national security had begun to be transformed, however, because the outsiders had established new ground rules for interpreting the data. The "new orthodoxy" rejected as a fundamental principle the proposition that Soviet leaders felt threatened by U.S. weapons development. Such "mirror-imaging," as Nitze called it, was ruled out from the start. The basic premise was that the Soviets were and remain *different*. The idea that the Soviet nuclear buildup could even in part be explained "on the ground that the Russians had a lot of catching up to do" or that "they had to consider the Chinese threat" was dismissed by Professor Richard Pipes as appeasement. When Soviet specialists, such as Marshall Shulman, the senior adviser on the Soviet Union to the Secretary of State, tried to offer contextual analyses of Soviet behavior, they were written off as apologists. There was an insidious "culture of appeasement," Podhoretz warned, that had infected the elite much like the mood in Neville Chamberlain's Britain when timid intellectuals made excuses for Hitler's rearmament.

The second battle in the war against détente was a personal attack against Paul Warnke, whom President Carter in February 1977 had named director of the Arms Control and Disarmament Agency and SALT negotiator. A widely circulated anonymous memorandum prepared by two staff members of the Coalition for a Democratic Majority who subsequently joined the Committee on the Present Danger charged Warnke with advocating "unilateral abandonment by the U.S. of every weapons system which is subject to negotiation at SALT." The nominee's suggestion that in its arms procurement the U.S. "try a policy of restraint, while calling for matching restraint from the Soviet Union" was equated with unilateral disarmament. "The imbalance between his vehement criticism of U.S. policy and relative silence about Soviet activities," a charge reminiscent of those leveled at antiwar critics in the Vietnam era, was "remarkable." While the anonymous memorandum challenged his patriotism, Paul Nitze attacked his judgment before the

Senate Foreign Relations Committee. Warnke's views were "absolutely asinine"; indeed, they verged on the "screwball, arbitrary, and fictitious." Recognizing that Warnke had "certain abilities as an advocate," he charged that "at least with respect to defense matters, these do not include clarity or consistency of logic."

An Emergency Coalition Against Unilateral Disarmament was organized at the offices of the Coalition for a Democratic Majority under the chairmanship of General Graham to campaign against the appointment. The steering committee included key representatives of ultra-right organizations: James G. Roberts, executive Director of the American Conservative Union; Howard Phillips, national director of the Conservative Caucus; and Paul Weyrich, director of the Committee for Survival of a Free Congress, who, according to *Peddlers of Crisis,* "sent out 600,000 letters urging voters to lobby their senators against Warnke." The objective of the campaign, as Senator Henry Jackson explained it, was to "weaken Warnke as an international negotiator to the point of uselessness by holding the vote in his favor to sixty or less." (Ratification of the SALT II treaty would take sixty-seven votes.) The hawkish coalition succeeded. Warnke was confirmed as SALT negotiator by a vote of fifty-eight to forty.

The third battle waged by the committee for the restoration of Cold War strategy and attitude was the fight over the SALT II treaty itself. Even before the treaty was signed in June 1979, the anti-SALT campaign led by the Committee on the Present Danger in alliance with the American Security Council had gathered enough momentum to force the Administration onto the defensive. They hammered away at the basic themes: the U.S. was already second to Russia; SALT would tie our hands; the treaty expressed the failure of nerve of an elite unprepared to strive for the military superiority the nation needed.

The American Security Council and its offshoot, the Co-alition for Peace Through Strength, carried out the lobbying activities, using the analyses prepared by the committee. In September 1978 the Coalition launched a $2-million drive to defeat the treaty. The campaign successfully focused attention on the critics' definition of the issues rather than the Administration's. Carter had come in stressing the point that security involved much more than the arms race with the Russians, a race that no one could win in any event. At Notre Dame's commencement on May 22, 1977, he had proclaimed an end to the "inordinate fear of Communism [that] led us to embrace any dictator who joined us in our fear." Step by step he gave ground to his attackers. The goal of eliminating nuclear weapons was never mentioned. There was no echo even of Kissinger's rhetoric of a "generation of peace." By the end of 1977 Secretary of Defense Harold Brown was assuring the National Security Industrial Association, "We will not be outgunned. We will not be bullied. We will not be coerced." The development of MX, the largest and costliest missile program in history, was ordered. Presidential Directive 18 called for an expanded conventional-arms program, including a "rapid development force" designed for quick military operations in the Middle East. The President continued to defend SALT, but the emphasis was now on the restrictions on further Soviet buildup it provided and the opportunities it offered to add to the U.S. strike force.

Still the attack on the Administration for neglecting the nation's defenses continued. In March 1978, at Wake Forest College, President Carter promised to match the Soviets in military spending. In his first budget, instead of the $5- to $7-billion cut promised in the campaign, he proposed a real increase of 3 percent a year. But the Committee on the Present Danger was not assuaged and stepped up its campaign. During the SALT hearings its members testified on seventeen different occasions before the Armed Services Committees and the Senate Foreign Relations Committee, participated in 479 TV and radio programs, and distributed 200,000 pamphlets, most of them written by Paul Nitze. In 1979, the American Security Council spent $3 million to defeat SALT II, and the American Conservative Union spent about $1.8 million.

The White House kept retreating before the barrage. By December 12, 1979, two weeks before the Soviet invasion of Afghanistan, Carter had ordered a land-based missile for West Europe capable of reaching the Soviet Union, a new "strategic" weapon, according to the Soviets, that violated SALT II. He had promised in a speech before the Business Council to increase defense spending at least 5 percent a year, and he had sent the Secretary of Defense to China to discuss "cooperation." Terming the Afghanistan invasion "the most serious threat to world peace since the Second World War," President Carter enunciated a "doctrine" that promised the use of force to protect U.S. interests in the Persian Gulf. Having vetoed one bill because it authorized a nuclear aircraft carrier, he signed another that did the same thing, and also reversed himself under pressure on military pay and benefits. By the opening of the Republican convention, Harold Brown, who in February 1977 announced that the new Administration would start to redeem its promise to cut the budget, charged, "When this administration took office, we inherited a military posture and a defense budget that simply had not kept pace." So far had the debate on national security shifted in four years that despite Carter's huge budget increases and belligerent rhetoric, Ronald Reagan accused him of making a "shambles" of the nation's defenses and of being "totally oblivious" to the Soviet drive for world domination. On November 4, 1980, Ronald Reagan was elected in a landslide. The world view of the Committee on the Present Danger, it now appeared, was national policy.

CHAPTER 4

Vietnam Syndrome?

In December 1979, President Carter said that he had learned more about the Soviets in the week they invaded Afghanistan than in his entire previous career and left the impression that his dramatic shift of rhetoric and policy with respect to national security was somehow attributable to that particular aggressive act. However, except for the grain embargo, the Olympic boycott, and an explicit threat of nuclear war if the Soviets moved into the Persian Gulf, the Administration's tougher policy was already being implemented before the Soviets used tanks to install Babrak Karmal as their man in Kabul. The campaign to dramatize the Russian threat had already succeeded. In the wake of the hostage crisis, unprecedented domestic inflation, the decline of the dollar, and growing tension with allies in Europe and Japan, many Americans felt that the foundations of security were collapsing. The anodyne for a growing sense of powerlessness was muscle-flexing. For the members of the Committee on the Present Danger, America's troubles were directly attributable to years of neglect of military power. Now at last the "Vietnam syndrome"—a deliberately disquieting term for a pathological condition that supposedly inhibited the United States from making effective use of force—had been overcome. There was a new consensus that America was declining in power. The remedy was to restore military might to restore American confidence. Then others would stop pushing us around. All this expressed what Cyrus Vance, in a speech at Harvard in June 1980, two months after his resignation as Secretary of State, called "nostalgia for the days when the U.S. had enormously greater influence in the world."

But the connection between military weakness and America's "retreat," as Richard Nixon called it, was not examined. The unstated assumption of the campaigners for rearmament and confrontation was that a tougher U.S. stance in the post-Vietnam years would have preserved American power. The questions Norman Angell had raised seventy years before about the relations between force and power were ignored in the political debate. As the new hawkish consensus took shape, the fundamental idea that force could in one way or another be translated into power stood unchallenged. It was now fashionable to note that only the United States was limited in the use of military power, and that was only because of its squeamishness, over-developed moral sensibilities, or cowardice. Neither the Russians, the Cubans, nor anyone else practiced unilateral "moral disarmament," and therefore they could make effective use of homicidal technology to advance their national interest.

The events of the last five years are difficult to squeeze into such a mold. The definition of an effective foreign policy, Henry Kissinger argued in a speech before the American Society of Newspaper Editors in April 1980, is that "somewhere, somehow, the United States must show that it is capable of rewarding a friend or penalizing an opponent." By that definition the nation must be able to use its military power to damage an adversary without inflicting great wounds on itself. The misuse of force—either by bluffing and having the bluff called or by undertaking a specific mission and failing—does not stem the decline of power. It accelerates the decline.

The American war in Indochina, like the French war before it, and the seventeen-day Chinese war after it, failed to achieve its stated objective. But, more seriously, the effort to stabilize South Vietnam by military means exacted political, economic, and social costs which the nation is still paying. Lyndon Johnson's insistence that the nation fight a $150-billion war and build a Great Society simultaneously, all without raising taxes, introduced an inflationary virus into what had been a remarkably inflation-free economy. Financing the distant war upset the balance of payments and led to the weakening of the dollar; the nations of Europe refused to subsidize the war, by simply rejecting payment in dollars they neither needed nor wanted. All this portended a new and more modest economic status for the United States, the clearest evidence of a real decline in power.

The social consequences within the United States, the growing lack of support for the political parties, the decline of confidence in government and in other institutions, the shakiness of the social consensus needed to govern—all are more difficult to measure. But the Johnson-Nixon years were utterly dominated by the Vietnam War, and the trauma remains. After reiterating for a dozen years that the United States could not accept failure because its prestige would suffer, the number-one nation did lose some of its aura of invincibility.

None of this elicits much debate now. Everyone is aware of the costs of the failure. The disagreement remains over whether the effort was "noble," as Ronald Reagan put it, and over whether the war could have been won by the employment of more extreme military measures. Walt Rostow, Lyndon Johnson's national-security adviser, believes that an invasion of North Vietnam could have turned defeat into victory. The subsequent Chinese invasion does not lend much support for that proposition. The Soviet invasion of Afghanistan is one more piece of evidence that suppressing guerrilla movements with large modern armies is easier to suggest than to accomplish. The main reason why the U.S. was unable to apply enough military force in Vietnam was that the American people did not believe that their stake in the outcome warranted the sacrifices that were demanded. There was indeed a failure of will. A crucial issue raised by the Vietnam War and not settled by it, is whether the United States could fight a war someplace else where the stakes were obviously higher, such as the Middle East, and elicit enough popular support to remain a democracy.

When is force useful and when isn't it? How much is enough to do that which holds reasonable promise of being effective? It is worth examining the major instances in which force has been used since Vietnam with these questions in mind.

America's first experience with the political uses of military power in the post–Vietnam War world occurred exactly twelve days after the fall of Saigon. The merchant ship *Mayaguez* was seized by the Cambodian government forces in the early afternoon of May 12, 1975, in an area claimed by the Cambodians as their territorial waters. During the previous ten days the Cambodians had stopped about twenty-five ships in the same area. They issued a communiqué disclaiming any intention of detaining the ship permanently. "We only wanted to know the reason for its coming and to warn it against violating our waters again."

Calling the seizure "an act of piracy," President Ford issued a twenty-four-hour ultimatum. At dawn the next day, while the crew was being transferred to the Cambodian mainland on a fishing vessel escorted by Cambodian patrol craft, U.S. aircraft began an air strike against the convoy. The captain of the *Mayaguez* described what happened:

They did everything that was possible without blowing us out of the water to try to get this boat to turn around and take us back to the ship.

If we were strafed or bombed once, we were bombed a hundred times by our jets. Ten foot forward of our bow light. Rockets and machine gun fire. When they saw that was not going to work, two jets overflew the boat from bow to stern approximately 70 feet above us and they tear gassed us.

. . . After a half hour passed and we were still going we were gassed a second time. I don't know whether it was tear gas or nausea gas, but everybody on the ship vomited, skin was burning, a couple of men were struck by shrapnel.*

In the early evening of May 14, the Cambodians told Captain Miller that he and the crew were free, and they gave the Americans a small boat with which to return to the *Mayaguez*. Fearing another attack from his own countrymen, the captain waited ten and a half hours until it was daylight. When they were twenty minutes under way and the Cambodian radio had already broadcast the news of their release, a U.S. naval force comprised of four destroyers, a guided-missile frigate, and a supply ship commenced an assault on Cambodia. A 15,000-pound bomb, the largest conventional explosive bomb in the U.S. arsenal at the time, was dropped on the tiny island of Koh Tang, where U.S. officials suspected the crew was being held. This curious rescue tactic was supplemented by an assault landing of two hundred Marines on Koh Tang and the bombing of the airport and of an oil refinery on the mainland. In the mission to rescue thirty crewmen who had already been released, forty-one Marines died.

This unnecessary human sacrifice produced a short term

* *Newsweek,* May 26, 1975, pp. 20, 21.

political success for the Ford Administration. The President's popularity index jumped ten points; 51 percent of the American people, according to a Gallup poll, approved of the military action. "This use of force was popular," one study of the *Mayaguez* incident concluded. "It was viewed as a partial vindication for the earlier losses in Indochina." * President Ford interpreted the brief episode of overkill as "a clear indication that we are not only strong, but we have the will and capability of moving." Secretary Kissinger stated that "the impact ought to make it clear that there are limits beyond which the U.S. cannot be pushed." Neither European nor Japanese leaders nor newspapers anywhere outside the United States were much impressed by the show of resolve, and the matter was quickly forgotten. Five years later the U.S. was supporting the Cambodian regime in crucial votes at the U.N.

Within a few weeks the United States was presented what Henry Kissinger believed was another opportunity "to show that it is capable of rewarding a friend or penalizing an opponent." Between November 1975 and March 1976 about 18,000 Cuban troops arrived in Angola to support the Soviet-aided MPLA in its struggle against two other U.S.- and Chinese-supported guerrilla groups for control of the recently liberated Portuguese colony. (According to Cuban estimates, at one time it had 36,000 troops in Angola.) By all accounts Cuba's military intervention was decisive to the outcome. At a critical moment the U.S. Congress refused to authorize covert assistance for the FNLA and UNITA, the two anti-Soviet groups it had been secretly aiding for a number of years. This failure of nerve, according to now familiar criticism, a product of the "Vietnam syndrome," handed an important Cold War victory to the Russians.

Cuba had sent troops abroad before—600–700 men to

* Robert R. Simmons, "Case Studies: The *Pueblo, EC 121,* and the *Mayaguez* Incidents."

Yemen and 500–750 armored troops to Syria in 1973—but although it had been providing arms and training for the MPLA since 1965, never before had it sent an expeditionary force on such a scale. The U.S. began shipping arms to the FNLA in July 1974, and the following year the "40 Committee," the senior U.S. officials charged with overseeing covert operations, increased its secret aid substantially. The struggle of the various Angolan factions to control their country was now an international war. Zaire sent 1,200 troops, and the FNLA and UNITA turned to South Africa for aid. In June 1975, when a substantial foreign intervention was already under way, 230 Cuban advisers arrived in Angola.

On July 17, the "40 Committee" authorized "Operation Feature," a program to recruit mercenaries for the Angola fighting and to send $32 million in armaments to be used against MPLA. (At about the same time the Gulf Oil Company was making its quarterly payment to the MPLA on its oil leases, which amounted to about three times the budget of the CIA operation. Cuban troops moved in to guard the Gulf refinery at Kabinda and remain to this day.) In August, South African troops crossed the frontier in support of an FNLA offensive and opened training bases for the FNLA and UNITA in Namibia and southern Angola. By late October, South Africa had launched "Operation Zulu," a 5,000-troop assault that advanced five hundred kilometers up the coast in a little over one week. At this point MPLA asked for Cuban combat troops, and the first battalion was airlifted to Luanda, the capital, on November 8. In a recent University of California monograph, "Cuba's Policy in Africa, 1959–1980," Professor William M. LeoGrande describes what happened:

> By mid-December the South African advance in the south had been halted, and the MPLA-Cuban forces had

gone over to the offensive against the FNLA-Zairean forces on the northern front. When the U.S. Congress prohibited further U.S. aid to the FNLA or UNITA, South Africa withdrew its troops to the border, charging that the United States had defaulted on its pledge to provide whatever military assistance was required to defeat the MPLA. Without the South Africans, UNITA quickly disintegrated as a fighting force. By early February, Cuba and the MPLA were able to concentrate their forces in the north, and within a few weeks the FNLA was in full retreat across the border, seeking refuge in Zaire. The collapse of UNITA and the FNLA was so rapid that by mid-March Castro and Neto were able to agree to a schedule for Cuban troop withdrawals.

The Angola intervention was a crucial symbolic moment in the postwar period. But what did it symbolize? It was not, as commonly alleged, a proxy war fought by the Soviet Union with Cuban troops. Secretary of State Kissinger told a *New York Times* reporter in February 1976 that the Cubans made their own decision. In his semiauthorized account from the Cuban perspective, the novelist Gabriel García Marquez says that the Soviet Union was not even consulted in advance of the decision. Although that is hard to believe given Cuba's dependence on the U.S.S.R., the record does suggest, as Professor LeoGrande's study puts it, that throughout the summer of 1975 "Cuba and the USSR appeared to be making independent decisions about their aid to the MPLA." The Soviets turned down a request to send advisers in August and proceeded much more cautiously than the Cubans.

The Soviets and the Cubans operated independently in Angola because they had different interests. The Soviets, eager to preserve détente, more concerned with economic and strategic objectives than the more ideological Cubans, exhibited more caution. Indeed, the Cubans in the late 1960s stepped up their commitment to "revolutionary internationalism" exactly because the Soviets appeared to be weakening in theirs. Chinese arms and instructors for the FNLA and the South African intervention brought the Cubans and the Soviets together. After the victory, Cuban and Soviet interests again diverged. In 1977 the Soviet Union had advance knowledge of a coup against Agostinho Neto, the MPLA leader, by a political opponent who favored closer alignment with the U.S.S.R., but the Soviets did not warn Neto. Cuban forces, however, directly helped to suppress the coup. Soviet-Angolan relations understandably cooled.

The "Vietnam syndrome" indeed operated in the case of Angola. Influential members of Congress blocked the proposed covert intervention because they believed that it could not succeed. The local forces on which the United States was relying just as in South Vietnam were weak; they would need repeated and increasing infusions of military aid. Once the prestige of the United States was sufficiently engaged, there would be considerable pressure to send in U.S. troops to stave off defeat. With the fall of Saigon a fresh memory, there was little inclination to take such a risk.

For military power to work, the use of force must be sufficient either to compel an opponent to do something or desist from doing something or at least to create for the user a properly intimidating image. For any such success there must be a fit between the military measures taken and the political situation to which they are directed. Military power is by no means useless, but its usefulness is limited by the context within which it is employed. It is a key that fits only certain locks. In the case of Angola the Cubans had the right key and the United States did not. Of course, the United States was in a position to airlift a much bigger force to Angola than any Cuban force, and the South Africans who would have joined the operation had the only first-class army on the continent. It was South Africa's participation on the other side, however, that lent legitimacy to the Cuban effort. Exactly because Cuba's motives were ideological, not geopolitical, because she had built up a long record of sending teachers, technicians, and doctors as well as soldiers to Africa, and because of their common racial heritage—Cuba has a large black population—the Cuban expeditionary force was accepted even by anti-Communist pro-Western African states. In May 1978 Kenneth D. Kaunda, President of Zambia, declared, "I am not sure there is a single Cuban on the African continent who has not been invited by some member of the continent. So long as this is the case, it is not easy to condemn their presence." Leslie Harriman, the ambassador to the United Nations from Nigeria, perhaps the most pro-Western black African nation, also defended the Cubans: "Cubans have never attacked any sovereign state or crossed an internationally recognized boundary. What they have done is to assist oppressed people gain their self-determination from colonial masters." The United States had little chance to make effective use of its military power in the struggle for Angola not only because of the domestic political climate in the U.S. but also because of African sentiment.

In the ensuing Ethiopian war the Cubans again tried their key, but this time with mixed success. Before the Ethiopian revolution which deposed Emperor Haile Selassie in February 1974, the Cubans had had little contact with the Horn of Africa. In the first two years after the coup by Ethiopian officers, Cuba sent several hundred military technicians to Somalia, a country they would soon fight on behalf of the Ethiopians. It was at the time a self-proclaimed "Marxist-Leninist" state and a Soviet client. Meanwhile the Ethiopian revolution was lurching to the left. In November 1974, the chairman of the provisional Military Administrative Council and fifty-nine other officers were executed for allegedly plotting with the U.S. to unseat the revolution. The meeting of the Council on February 3, 1977, degenerated into a shoot-out. The radical faction headed by Mengistu Haile-Mariam was the winner in the bloodbath. Ethiopia was proclaimed a "Marxist-Leninist" country. The Dergue, as the government is called, now faced an ultra-left student group bent on assassinating its officials, a secessionist war in the Ogaden region, aided by Somalia, and an Eritrean rebellion aided by Sudan, Egypt, and Saudi Arabia. To complicate matters further, one of the three Eritrean secessionist groups was also Marxist.

The Soviet Union tried unsuccessfully to mediate the dispute over Ogaden between two of its clients. Ethiopia, only a short time before the site of an important U.S. intelligence-gathering base, at Kagnew, and the most pro-American country in the region, was the greater prize. Once the Dergue had ousted the U.S. military mission, the Soviets began to supply the Ethiopians with arms, and in May 1977 the Cubans sent military advisers. At this point, the Somalis, fearing the Ethiopian arms buildup, attacked in Ogaden. Saudi Arabia offered the Somalis $350 million to break with the Soviets, and Secretary of State Vance hinted that the U.S. would also provide arms. The Somalis, having achieved considerable military success—some forty thousand of their troops were now engaged—broke relations with Cuba and expelled the Soviet military mission. On the strength of U.S. and British offers of "defensive" arms, they expected tacit support for their invasion. But this was a miscalculation. Western arms did not arrive. The Cubans sent in seventeen thousand regulars. As William M. Leo-Grande concludes in his study on Cuba's policy in Africa, there was considerably more cooperation between the Soviets and the Cubans in Ethiopia than there had been in Angola:

In Ethiopia, Cuban troops arrived not in converted freighters but in Soviet troop transports. Soviet military advisors numbered over a thousand, and they played a central role in planning and commanding the Ogaden campaign. In Angola the role of Soviet personnel had been only marginal. Soviet-Cuban cooperation in Ethiopia was so close, in fact, that Soviet pilots were apparently assigned air defense duty in Cuba to ease the shortage of Cuban pilots, many of whom were flying combat mission in the Ogaden. The Somalis, short on supplies, proved to be no match for the Cubans. Using standard Soviet assault tactics, a Cuban-Ethiopian force captured the key city of Jijiga in early March, and the Somalis fell back across the border.

The U.S. never aided Somalia, because Somalia was the aggressor, a fact accepted by such pro-Western African states as Nigeria and Kenya who supported Ethiopia despite their ideological antipathy for the Dergue. The U.S. hints about military aid may have confused the Somalis, but the opportunity for successful U.S. military intervention in the Horn of Africa was limited. Once again, it was not that the U.S. lacked a rapid deployment force capable of matching seventeen thousand Cubans—Marine divisions and the 82nd Airborne Division were available—but that the political context in which force could be successfully used was lacking.

The Cubans succeeded in beating back the Somalis, but now their military operations encountered some serious political problems. The Cubans had become much closer collaborators of the Russians. But the Soviets had decided to support Mengistu in his effort to crush the Eritrean insurgency, while Castro called it an "internal problem" and promised not to intervene militarily. But although Castro continued to urge a political solution, his troops in the Ogaden made it possible for Mengistu to continue a war Castro opposed. This reality was not lost on other African countries, who saw the Soviet support in behalf of the bloody Dergue less a commitment to liberation than a geopolitical power grab.

Ethiopia has become a bit of a quagmire for Cuba. Relations with the Dergue have been rocky. In 1978 the Cubans arranged for the return to Ethiopia of Negedu Gobezi, a potential rival of Mengistu, and Mengistu expelled the Cuban ambassador. The protracted war and internal violence in Ethiopia has robbed Cuba of some of the prestige in Africa it earned in Angola. It is now regarded as more of a Soviet agent despite its continued differences with the U.S.S.R. over Eritrea. As LeoGrande puts it, "while Angola increased respect for both Cuba's power and its motives, Ethiopia added little to the former while detracting considerably from the latter." Progress toward normalization of relations with the United States was stopped dead. Canada canceled its aid. The Ethiopian intervention reinforced the growing perception among American national-security officials of a Soviet-Cuban challenge in an "arc of crisis" that extended from Africa to the Middle East. These perceptions contributed in turn to the overreaction of American politicians to the Soviet "combat brigade," two to three thousand Soviet troops that had been in Cuba since 1962 whose presence was now declared by President Carter in a spectacular show of impotence to be "unacceptable." They are of course still there. Cuba's intervention increased her dependence upon the Soviet Union, a condition Castro had been seeking to modify. The economic burden of the expeditionary force in Africa has been heavy, and in the opinion of U.S. intelligence analysts it has aggravated the economic problems that have brought more than 100,000 refugees to Florida.

CHAPTER 5

The Limits of
Military Power

In the early years following withdrawal from Indochina, the U.S. considered but decided against the commitment of substantially increased military forces in Africa. In 1978 the Carter Administration did supply the transport planes that enabled Belgian and French paratroopers to recapture the copper mines of Kolwezi in the Shaba province of Zaire from an invading force launched from Angola. The invaders were members of a Shaba independence movement, a group supported by the U.S. in the early 1960s. The White House accused Cuba of being behind the invasion, and when the State Department, the CIA, and the Foreign Affairs Committees of Congress all concluded that the evidence of Cuban involvement was scanty, the Carter Administration retorted that even if Cuba did not plot the invasion it could have done more to prevent it. At about the same time the CIA proposed a new covert-assistance plan to aid UNITA in Angola, but Senator Dick Clark, chairman of the Senate Foreign Relations Subcommittee on Africa, made the plans public and they were dropped.

In the Middle East the efforts to shore up U.S. interests with military power were much greater, but the results were equally inconclusive. After the Arab boycott of 1974, and the gas lines, inflation, unemployment, and panic that accompanied the petroleum cutoff, it was now self-evident that the U.S. had "vital interests" in the Persian Gulf. Every Secretary of Defense since the Nixon administration has said that we would go to war to protect our access to oil. In 1979 Soviet Ambassador Anatoly Dobrynin was summoned to the State Department to be informed that the U.S. considers the Persian Gulf an area of "vital U.S. interest," and in January 1980 President Carter proclaimed the "Carter Doctrine," which made the same point in a more public way.

No one doubts that vital interests of the United States are at stake in the Middle East. The question is how these can be protected by military power. There have been two aspects to American strategy. The first has been to make clear to the Soviet Union that a major attack on the oil lifeline would run the risk of a nuclear war. Pentagon plans to implement the Carter Doctrine with a nuclear "trip-wire" were intentionally leaked to *The New York Times:* The small forces the U.S. intended to put into the region were not expected to defend against Russian hordes but to symbolize the Administration's determination to use nuclear weapons if "necessary." The limited use of nuclear weapons, the Secretary of Defense himself had said, risked an escalation to a "full-scale nuclear exchange," which would, of course, vaporize the oil along with the civilization that depended on it. This "credibility problem" could be minimized, Pentagon strategists argued, by introducing increased naval forces, and "pre-positioned" military supplies for use by a "rapid deployment force" that would be flown to the region in an emergency, and by establishing new bases in the area.

But this second line of defense had inherent difficulties, too. Under the Nixon Doctrine the U.S. had sold the Shah of Iran some $20 billion of sophisticated weaponry. He was to be the regional peacekeeper and conservator of American interests. Endowing the Shah was in fact an abdication of American power, for Mohammed Reza Pahlavi had his own pretensions and his own plans, some of which worked at cross purposes to American strategy. He was, for example, the most aggressive supporter among the oil producers of a major price hike in 1973. His own petty imperial plans kept much of the region stirred up. His interference in Afghanistan, according to Selig Harrison, a Carnegie Endowment scholar who has studied the events closely, set off the chain of circumstances that led to the Soviet invasion. He did, however, successfully crush a guerrilla war in Oman in 1973 which all the oil-consuming nations considered a service.

The huge shipment of arms to the Shah did not save him; indeed, the conspicuous American military presence in Iran —at the high point some forty thousand technicians were there—catalyzed the rebellion and by highlighting the Shah's American dependence gave the Islamic Revolution an anti-American cast it would not otherwise have had. The dramatic appearance of millions of the Ayatollah Khomeini's followers in the streets and the collapse of the Iranian military in the face of this phenomenon made a U.S. military intervention to save the Shah impractical. (The mission of General Robert Huyser to Teheran in January 1979 to persuade the Iranian generals to transfer their loyalty from the Shah to Prime Minister Bakhtiar added to the confusion and underscored American helplessness in the face of the revolution.)

With the collapse of America's strategy for the Persian Gulf, the Carter Administration sought an opportunity to make a show of strength. It was urged to do so by Saudi Arabia, a regime that relied on the U.S. for its internal security. The Saudi royal family was another huge recipient of American arms; the sheiks were now feeling vulnerable in the wake of the Shah's humiliating departure. A war in Yemen within weeks of the Shah's overthrow provided the occasion for a highly publicized U.S. military-assistance effort. On February 23, 1979, forces of North Yemen and South Yemen (another self-proclaimed "Marxist-Leninist" regime that has had Cuban advisers since 1973) clashed at the frontier. Military efforts of one sort or another to unify what both sides consider a single country have been going on since the British abandoned the area in 1967. An uneasy truce imposed by the Arab League had been in force since 1972, but in mid-1978 the situation deteriorated. An emissary from South Yemen to the President of North Yemen left with him a briefcase with a bomb in it which exploded and killed him. The assassination set off a struggle in South Yemen, and a faction considered more pro-Soviet came to power. The Saudis provided North Yemen with several hundred million dollars' worth of arms they had purchased from the U.S., and the Carter Administration agreed to replace the Saudi stockpile. In South Yemen the strength of the Cuban advisory mission was doubled. For the Carter Administration the seven hundred Cubans and the pro-Russian sympathies of the South Yemenis made the remote internal battle over the political direction of Yemen somehow part of the same regional war that had spread across Angola and Ethiopia.

Within two weeks of the border clashes the Carter Administration shipped to Saudi Arabia $400 million worth of miliary equipment intended for Yemen, including F-5E aircraft for which Administration officials admitted the North Yemenis had no pilots. Dozens of U.S. training personnel and advisers and shipments of spare parts were promised over the next two years. The White House made much of its decision to dispatch this equipment on an emergency basis. It was to be the proving ground for a new tough policy in the "arc of crisis." Richard Burt reported for *The New York*

Times that "Mr. Carter's decision is a departure in his Administration's use of military force—it is said to reflect his interest in showing American concern for the security of the Persian Gulf and the Middle East." A high White House official declared, "We've got a brush fire going at a time and in a place where a great deal is at stake." As a show of resolve the Yemeni military-aid program backfired. The regime in North Yemen, which U.S. intelligence estimates had predicted would not last six months because of domestic opposition, did survive, but by late 1979 it had turned to the Soviet Union for military aid.

A few weeks after the U.S. arms were shipped to the Saudis for transshipment to North Yemen the two Yemeni states suddenly stopped fighting and signed another agreement to proceed toward eventual unification. The Saudis, who feared the prospect of a united Yemen 7 million strong —roughly their own population—then slowed up on deliveries of the U.S. equipment. The North Yemeni Army, it turned out, accustomed to Russian equipment since the 1960s, was finding it difficult to use U.S. weaponry anyway. The traditional Yemeni hostility toward Saudi Arabia—the Saudis annexed three Yemeni provinces in 1934 and are blamed for the assassination of the popular President Ibrahim al-Hamdi in 1977—caused the Yemenis to look toward the Russians. The Soviets, according to the North Yemeni Prime Minister, contrary to their usual practice, were rather gentle and cooperative in proposing military aid with few conditions. By the end of the year, ten MIG-21s, one hundred T-55 tanks, and more than one hundred advisers had arrived in North Yemen.

The Carter Administration takes credit for the truce in the war of the Yemens, but the U.S. aid program clearly had a quite different effect from what was intended. President Ali Abdullah Saleh accused both the U.S. and the Soviet Union of playing a "superpower game" in the region. He was determined, and apparently still is, to balance Saudi-U.S. influence with Soviet aid. (In March 1980 the Saudis agreed to train the North Yemenis in the use of Soviet weapons if the Russian advisers would go home.) The U.S. involvement may well have encouraged a settlement as an alternative to an East–West confrontation over Yemen. But the prestige of the U.S. was hardly advanced by having the new client turn to Moscow for arms within a year of having been designated a strategic country in dire need of protection from the Soviets. By talking about an "arc of crisis" that embraced quite separate national and tribal struggles, each with its own long history, the Administration deceived itself. Neither Africa nor the Middle East is easily fitted into a Cold War mold and certainly not into the same mold. There are no more radical states or fiercer anti-Communist ones anywhere, but the ideological considerations vie with historic antipathies and geopolitical rivalries that stir ancient passions at a deeper level.

After the Soviet invasion of Afghanistan the Administration advertised its plans for an increased military presence in the Persian Gulf. It accelerated preparations for a rapid deployment force—specially trained units for a quick strike into the Persian Gulf or other strategic Third World regions. The 180,000-man Marine Corps already has such a mission, as does the 82nd Airborne Division, a part of which is on continuous alert and can be flown anywhere in the world within twenty-four hours. Three weeks before the Afghanistan invasion the Carter Administration announced a $9-billion five-year program to increase the quick-reaction capabilities of U.S. military forces.

In the Vietnam era, rapid deployment was not an appealing idea; Senator Richard Russell, chairman of the Armed Services Committee, said that if the Army had equipment that would enable it to go places and do things, that is exactly what it would do. The "half-war" in Vietnam, as it was designated by Pentagon planners who seek to keep the U.S. prepared to fight a "war and a half" at all times, seemed to be enough. Now the political mood is different. A rapid deployment force scarcely arouses controversy, and the U.S. Army is making major preparations for desert warfare. As Major General Paul X. Kelley put it, the U.S. was entering the 1980s "with a sharper focus on the Third World. . . . We would do well to sharpen that focus before we let the thing slip through our fingers."* As another Pentagon official put it, "When you begin looking at the mid-eighties, we aren't talking about barbarians with knives. We're talking about pretty well-armed countries. . . . The problem is that a lot of the crisis regions are right at the Soviet Union's back door, so who moves first is very important."†

In 1979, a few days before the Soviet invasion of Afghanistan, Zbigniew Brzezinski, the National Security Adviser, was telling visitors, according to *The New York Times,* that "the nation has finally thrown off aversion to military spending and possible intervention abroad that was the legacy of Vietnam. He attributes the change partly to time and partly to a new perception of Soviet and Cuban 'adventurism' in the third world. He also feels that this has been reinforced by the situation in Iran, where Americans see their vital interests involved. . . ." Senator Gary Hart, agreeing that the public mood had changed, attributed the new willingness to support interventionary forces to the train of events "beginning with the fall of Saigon five years ago leading to the seizure of the hostages in Teheran."‡

Public frustration about the turn of events was understandable. The world was becoming more and more of an

---

* "U.S. to Speed Rapid-Response Capability by Military at 5-Year Cost of $9 Billion," *Wall Street Journal,* December 6, 1979.
† *Ibid.*
‡ Terence Smith, "Carter's Plans for Arms Rise," *The New York Times,* December 14, 1979.

unmanageable place. The impulse to put one's foot down was powerful, but where to put it without stumbling was by no means clear. None of the crises that arose since the fall of Saigon could be attributed to a lack of U.S. military personnel and equipment, certainly not to a lack of nuclear missiles. Something was happening in the late twentieth century to change traditional relationships between the capacity to make war and the ability to exercise political power. Big wars were obsolete even before the advent of nuclear weapons, as Norman Angell had noted, because technology and economics had substantially eradicated the difference between victory and defeat. But "brushfire wars," military-aid programs, rescue missions, and other uses of force now also appeared to be increasingly counterproductive; that is, it was becoming harder to translate battlefield success into increased stability, increased security, or any other value which the sacrifice of blood and treasure was supposed to achieve. How and where to apply military force without doing excessive damage or taking excessive risks was increasingly a problem. Even where a military or paramilitary intervention did accomplish short-term objectives it did not produce long-term stability. Guatemala, the scene of an efficient CIA-organized coup against the Arbenz government in 1954, is now on the brink of civil war. The political polarization of Central America and the Caribbean, a generation later, is dangerously advanced, and U.S. options to influence the outcome, with either political or military means, are considerably reduced.

The prognosis for the rapid deployment force, at least with respect to assuring the continued flow of oil, was not encouraging. In a 1978 study for *Military Review* entitled "Foreign Energy Sources and Military Power," two army officers who had worked in the White House, Major Daniel W. Christman and Major Wesley K. Clark, concluded that "the use of force was not a feasible alternative to diplomacy [in the 1973 embargo] and will not be directly useful in similar confrontations in the future.'' Since 80 percent of Aramco workers are Arabs, the "threat of sabotage would require a continued presence by sizable American forces.'' Christman and Clark correctly observe that "even the support of the U.S. oil companies affected was highly problematical. U.S. intervention in one area would have left company assets in another area as hostage.'' Company interests are in long-term profitability. Since that interest is better served by siding with the local regimes than with a temporary force of occupying Marines, the political foundations for successful gunboat diplomacy are missing. "U.S. military force," they conclude, "will be ineffective in coercing petroleum-producing states to respond to America's wishes.'' A Congressional Research Service study by Colonel John Collins came to the same general conclusions.

U.S. military power has been a wasting asset for a generation. Despite the spectacular achievements of U.S. military technology and the maintenance of forces which in killing power are still "second to none," the nation can accomplish less with military might than in the past. The extraordinary failure of the Iranian rescue mission dramatized the misfit between the structure of American forces and the political-economic forces which they are supposed to tame. (It was a success only in relieving the Administration for a time of domestic political pressure.) According to the official Pentagon investigation, the extraordinary secrecy required for the mission interfered with sensible planning. If so, that was a problem inherent in the operation and not easily overcome. Even if the rescue mission had succeeded, more American lives would have been imperiled than would have been saved. The Iranians could have made hostages of or summarily executed the more than two hundred Americans still in Teheran. This was a key point—the necessity to mislead allies to preserve secrecy was another—that convinced

Cyrus Vance that the mission was so ill-conceived that he could not remain as Secretary of State.

The Russians, living in the same world, face the same constraints on the use of military power. After the Afghanistan invasion Secretary of Defense Brown declared that they are "an aging revolutionary movement" tempted to use force to offset a declining economy, waning ideological appeal, internal stresses, and a growing appetite for imported oil. There is evidence, he said, that the Soviets "intend to use their seven airborne divisions . . . as a major instrument for possible military operations beyond their borders."

Perhaps so. The most persistent form of "mirror-imaging" that goes on in both Washington and Moscow is a common view of the adversary. Each sees the other as a failed system kept alive as a world force by its military might. Despite all the social and economic problems besetting both capitalist and Communist nations, this ideologically based view is probably exaggerated, since it encourages each to underestimate the strength and stability of the other and to overemphasize the importance of the military competition in their relationship. It is true, however, that the Soviets have in recent years acquired military forces for countering U.S. interventions and for conducting their own. They are, as a recent review of the Soviet use of force by Stephen Kaplan puts it, still cautious about resorting to military action, but less so than in the past. Senator Richard Russell's logic applies also to the Russians. If a country invests heavily in military forces that can go places and do things, that is what the forces are likely to do.

But if the Soviets throw their traditional caution to the wind and step up the pace of military intervention abroad, it will not be because of the great political successes they have scored with military power in the postwar world. True, the extension of the traditional Russian Empire into Eastern Europe in the closing months of the Second World War was accomplished entirely with military power. But the efforts to keep it with an occupation force have involved enormous costs. The Soviet leaders have made it clear—in East Germany in 1953, in Hungary in 1956, in Czechoslovakia in 1968 —that they are prepared to pay the costs rather than lose the protective belt of "socialist" states in Eastern Europe. But the interventions led directly to a loss of power and prestige. They split the world Communist movement, exacerbated Russia's "loss" of China, gave rise to pro-NATO, anti-Soviet Communist parties in Western Europe, and irreparably damaged the appeal of Soviet ideology inside the Soviet Union and in the the Third World. These brutal acts of repression dramatized Soviet political and ideological weakness.

So also the aggression against Afghanistan. The intervention was an act of desperation and a political miscalculation. Afghanistan, the classic "Finlandized" country, had been a feudal monarchy which defined its foreign policy as not displeasing the Russians. From all indications, having a stable reactionary government on its borders suited the Soviet government. But a coup in 1978 brought to power in Kabul a group of self-styled Marxist army officers who looked to the Soviets for aid. The Kremlin invoked the Brezhnev Doctrine, a position originally taken at the time of Alexander Dubček's reformist government in Czechoslovakia, that once a country was initiated into the socialist camp the Soviet Union would not permit it to leave. Afghanistan, one of the most traditional, Islamic, and anti-Communist countries in the world, fiercely resisted the "revolution." The clumsy, brutal tactics of the regime in the pursuit of such policies as land reform and increased freedom for women aroused the whole country to arms. The Soviets moved in to prevent the establishment of an anti-Soviet state on the borders of its own Islamic provinces. The consequences for U.S.–Soviet relations were no doubt underestimated.

In a limited sense, Afghanistan has already become "Russia's Vietnam." With a large military force and the employment of brutal tactics against villages the Soviets manage to maintain shaky control of the capital and the principal highways—during the day. The resistance is waning, but it is by no means crushed. Even without substantial outside suppliers, fighting continues at a level sufficient to keep international attention periodically focused on the struggle. Soviet casualties are mounting. Extrication is difficult. If the troops leave without a compromise political settlement, an anti-Soviet regime on their borders will take power. If they stay, a debilitating war goes on. The Soviets are playing a political role reminiscent of the U.S. role in Vietnam, where American advisers consistently pressured the Saigon regime to broaden their support by becoming more liberal. In Afghanistan the Soviets are telling their clients to become more conservative, to make peace with the trading class, and to be gentler with the people.

Buying influence with arms has been at least as bad a bargain for the Soviets as for the Americans. Indeed, major recipients of military aid have become major antagonists. China, whose revolution Stalin aided, though not enthusiastically enough to suit Mao, now aims nuclear rockets at Soviet cities. Over seven years the Soviet Union delivered $1.34 billion in military aid to Indonesia, but in 1965 an anti-Communist military dictatorship massacred the cadres of the Indonesian Communist Party along with hundreds of thousands of others and broke off all relations with the Soviet Union. Egypt received $5 billion in Soviet aid and once had twenty thousand Russian military technicians. They were expelled in 1972, the debt was repudiated, local Communists were jailed, and Anwar Sadat's policy became expressly anti-Soviet. Iraq, after years of dependence on the Soviets for arms, has recently cooled toward the Soviet Union. One billion dollars in military aid and one thousand military advisers sent to Somalia counted for nothing once the Soviets decided to back Somalia's enemy, Ethiopia. The Somalis have offered the Soviet-built base at Berbera to the Americans. Even countries such as Angola and Mozambique, which are self-described "Marxist-Leninist" nations, both recipients of crucial Soviet aid in their liberation struggles, zealously guard their independence from the Soviet Union. Despite the continued effort by UNITA supported by South Africa to unseat the government, and continued dependence on Soviet military aid, the government of Angola rejected Soviet requests for deep-water naval facilities at Lobito and Luanda. Mozambique has also refused Soviet requests for base rights.

In one African country after another, the Soviet Union sought and failed to purchase reliable clients with military aid and advisers—Guinea, Algeria, Mali, and Sudan. In every one of them Soviet influence has declined. In the war years 1965–75 the Soviet Union shipped North Vietnam about $1 billion a year; today about $2 million worth of military and economic aid arrives every day. The Hanoi regime, which before 1965 was much more closely aligned to China than to Russia, is now increasingly dependent on the Soviets. Pham Van Dong, the Vietnamese Prime Minister, had wanted to pursue a "five-sided diplomacy" (Vietnam interacting with China, the Soviet Union, the U.S., and the Third World) once the war came to an end. The country would, he hoped, derive half its aid from the West so as to reduce dependence on the Soviets. Hanoi joined the Association of Southeast Asian Nations (branded an "imperialist creation" by the Soviet Union), the World Bank, the International Monetary Fund, and the Asian Development Bank, all Western capitalist institutions, but declined an invitation to become a member of the Soviet-dominated Council of Mutual Economic Assistance (COMECON) in 1976. Because of a disagreement over the payment of reparations, the U.S. refused to provide aid or to proceed with normalization of relations. In this situation Soviet leverage increased and Vietnam joined COMECON in June 1978 and signed a treaty of friendship and cooperation with the Soviet Union a few months later. The Soviets may acquire the huge American-built base at Camranh Bay, just as the U.S. is about to acquire the old Soviet base at Berbera. But if Vietnam's history is any indication, the recently reunified nation is too nationalistic and jealous of its independence to be a pliable client. Meanwhile, like Cuba, it continues to drain the Soviet treasury.

China carried out a seventeen-day war against Vietnam beginning on February 17, 1979, to "teach Vietnam a lesson." The Chinese successfully destroyed practically all economic, political, and military facilities within about twenty kilometers of the frontier before they withdrew. They severely damaged Vietnam's efforts to recover from the thirty years of war, but the economic cost to China was severe. Robert Barnett, former State Department Asian expert, estimates that the war set China's military modernization program back at least a year and cost several billions of dollars. If the purpose was to destroy the myth of Vietnamese invincibility, as Vice-Premier Den Xiaoping put it, or to discourage Hanoi's closer relations with Moscow, it did not succeed. The Vietnamese have not reduced their efforts to control Cambodia. The principal lesson the Chinese may have taught is that a huge Asian power can no more effectively control Vietnam with military might than the two Western powers who tried and failed over thirty years.

Perhaps the most successful use of military force by an industrial nation in the past five years has been France's African operations. The French successfully transported Moroccan troops to secure Shaba in Zaire in 1977, won a decisive battle in Chad the next year, saved the Mobutu regime with another intervention in Shaba, played a key role in the overthrow of the brutal regime in the Central African Empire, and intervened with some success in a war involving three of its allies in the western Sahara—Algeria, Morocco, and Mauritania. France is seeking to use military aid to stabilize the region and to preserve access to vital resources. Because its operations are less visible than those of the U.S. and the Soviet Union and are less costly because they are on a smaller scale, they appear to be relatively more effective. (None of the conflicts in which France has intervened in the last five years, however, is settled.) The biggest gainer of all from the use of violence in the last five years, it would seem, has been the Palestine Liberation Organization, which successfully employed terrorism to make the world take note of the Palestine problem. It may well be that in the contemporary world, the smaller and less established a brandisher of bombs is, the more advantage it can derive from its use.

The real debate on national security in the United States is between those who believe the nation has insufficient military power to create a world hospitable for American goods, American values, and the servicing of American needs and call for more guns, bombs, and tanks to do the job, and those who believe that the objective cannot be achieved with any quantity of military power. If it is to be achieved, it must be achieved in other ways. It is self-evident that the world is dangerous, unsettled, violent, and maddeningly unpredictable. The taking of hostages, the gratuitous insults in the U.N., the monumental ingratitude of petty clients, and the heavy-handed, often puzzling behavior of the Soviet Union all foster an impulse to reach for the gun. Yet when we do reach for the gun, it does not seem to work the way it used to work. Is this because something has happened to the American spirit, as the advocates of "get-tough" policies taunt, or because the world has changed?

When Albert Einstein observed at the dawn of the nuclear age that the power of the unleashed atom had changed everything "except our way of thinking," he was identifying only one of the revolutionary factors of contemporary life that have transformed politics. At least three others have changed the relationship between force and power even when civilization-threatening weapons are not involved.

The first is the coming into consciousness in the last two generations of billions of people who previously were objects rather than subjects of international politics. With the collapse of the old colonial empires and the birth of 150 "nations," it is no longer possible to settle the fate of hundreds of millions of people in Asia, Africa, and Latin America in a few chancelleries of Europe. Once a drawing-room drama, international politics has become an extravaganza with a cast of thousands—not just the new nations but also dissident groups and terrorist organizations which also have the power to make their presence felt. The rules for using violence have been changing—not the treaties regulating the use of force, which are usually honored in the breach, but the unspoken rules which actually guide political leaders. Into center stage have come ancient religious and tribal rivalries which make the organization of battle lines by the most powerful nations exceedingly difficult. Thus, arming Pakistan to fight the Russians in Afghanistan, a plausible if dangerous Cold War strategy, must be ruled out because Paks and Afghans cannot agree on their ancient border. Saudi Arabia no more than Iran can be an effective surrogate wielder of military power, because of old scores in the region not yet settled. When these ancient tensions and rivalries did not matter because the people who cared passionately about them had no international visibility, it was easier for great powers to ignore local conflicts in their rivalries with one another or, indeed, to exploit them.

In the early postwar years when the decolonization process was just under way, it was easier to organize the U.S. security system on the principle of anti-Communism. Despite the precipitous decline in the appeal of Communism over the last twenty years, or perhaps because of it, an international security system based on anti-Communism is unrealizable. For most people in the world neither the writings of Marx and Lenin, the virtues and deficiencies of the Soviet central planning system, nor the betrayed dreams of a classless society are the issues that define reality. Hitlerism was an easy target because there was only one Hitler, who gave every evidence of being a mad conqueror who had to be stopped. But some of the bloodiest wars of the past five years have been between nations calling themselves Communist—Cambodia and Vietnam, Vietnam and China—and the most plausible spark for a world war, some observers believe, is renewed fighting between the Soviet Union and China.

The enormous complexity of the contemporary world makes a simple security strategy obsolete. Violence, as Hannah Arendt put it in her extraordinary study, is politically effective only to the extent that its use is perceived as legitimate. Indeed, when it is seen as legitimate it does not need to be used much. As Britain found in India, once opposition grows to the point at which a colonial power must fight a war rather than a low-level police operation, the use of violence becomes illegitimate and ultimately ineffective. Modern war achieves its political purpose through its psychological impact. *Schrecklichkeit,* as the early German theorists of modern warfare called it, creates the power to regulate the political behavior of masses of people by intimidating leaders. For the strategy to work there must be effective command and control, as the military call it; that is, the leaders who are to be intimidated must have the ability to surrender docile populations to the conqueror. The present situation in Iran is but an extreme case of a more general condition—the

inability of political leaders even under severe threat to control popular passions or to pacify their own territory. In such
a situation the use of force from outside is ineffective for
achieving political purposes. In international relations it may
still be legitimate to "punish" an adversary, but not leader-
less crowds.

A second revolution has occurred in military technology.
The spread of nuclear weapons is already an accomplished
fact. According to the U.S. Arms Control and Disarmament
Agency, there will be enough "weapons-grade" nuclear ma-
terial moving about the planet in 1985 in addition to that
controlled by the acknowledged nuclear powers to make
twenty thousand Hiroshima-range nuclear weapons. South
Africa and Israel, two nations involved in a potential life-or-
death struggle over the next two decades, are presumed by
many intelligence agencies to have nuclear weapons already.
We now live in what the military historian Harvey A. De-
Weerd calls a "balkanized world," a world of small, poor,
but overmilitarized states struggling for power. It is, he says,
an "unmanageable" world and a dangerous one for the
United States because a local nuclear war can suck in the
great powers. Emphasizing the familiar point that generals
are always preparing for the last war, DeWeerd notes that
the next wars are not likely to be either a replay of the
Second World War in Europe, to which most of our conventional forces are addressed, or a military expedition in the
desert. They will be wars on the model of the Iraq–Iran
conflict. In the small wars of the future the belligerents will
be exceedingly hard to control by outside powers. Modern
weapons are now readily available on the international market. The U.S. itself has since World War II sold, lent, or
given away more than $100 billion of armaments. Of the fifty
largest U.S. industrial companies, thirty-two make or export
arms.

The purpose of arms shipments has been, as former Secretary of Defense James Schlesinger put it in 1975, "to maintain influence." "The degree of influence of the supplier is potentially substantial, and typically, those relationships are enduring," he declared in defending the massive arms shipments to the Shah and other Persian Gulf recipients. But the spread of military technology has had exactly the opposite effect. Rather than making the recipients dependent, it has turned out to be something of an equalizer. Poor, weak countries, though they may be hopelessly in debt and their populations may be starving, can and do conduct formidable military operations—against their own populations and against their neighbors. There is little the great powers can do about it. Recent advances in military technology favor the defense over the attacker. The cruiser or the aircraft carrier, the modern vehicles for international swaggering, are exceedingly vulnerable to shore-launched missiles of the sort that many Third World countries now have. The first thirty years of the postwar era were remarkably stable, in large part because the U.S. had something approaching a monopoly of military power. It had most of the world's nuclear weapons and had the only fighting force that could be dispatched to distant corners of the globe. In part because of the Soviet buildup, in part because of a worldwide arms buildup to which the U.S. has been by far the largest contributor, the world is much less amenable to being managed by American military power. This reality is reflected in the schizophrenic reaction of the Persian Gulf states who privately urge the United States to take a tougher military role in their area but, like Saudi Arabia, refuse to allow the U.S. to have a base on their territory. The base, the royal family knows, would arouse political opposition, domestic and foreign, and it could not save their regime. (Oman, smaller and weaker, was persuaded under considerable pressure, to provide base rights to the U.S.)

The third transformation in the relationship between force

and power has come about because of an escalation in the cost of military might. As weapons have become more complex, they have become more expensive. They require esoteric metals and esoteric skills to produce. The nature of warfare itself and the development of democratic consciousness have driven up manpower costs astronomically. In an all-out war to save the country from attack, men can be drafted and paid twenty-one dollars a month as they were in 1940. In a war for more obscure goals soldiers expect to be better paid, especially if the war appears to be more or less of a permanent fixture. In a democratic society the choice is either a draft that bows in the direction of universal service or a well-paid professional army. Since Vietnam the nation has chosen the latter, and the taxpayer has been paying heavily for it. Ironically, the cost of maintaining politically effective military forces has gone up, even though with inflation the pay is generally inadequate, while the cost of mass destruction has gone down. (From a cost-effectiveness standpoint, atomic bombs are a bargain.)

In the early 1950s the United States tripled the military budget in about eighteen months to make the point urged so passionately in NSC-68. The Korean War was the political occasion, but most of the buildup went to Europe as a symbol of U.S. global commitment. (No military leader at the time actually expected a Soviet attack.) As the French strategist Raymond Aron has pointed out, in the 1980s it would be impossible to repeat such a feat. The U.S. will spend over $1 trillion in the next five years just to maintain a 5 percent increase in military forces. The impact of military spending on the U.S. economy has, unaccountably, never been subjected to a full-scale examination by the National Security Council. But there are increasing indications that the economic costs of military power weaken the economy in specific ways and to that extent damage national security.

In the 1950s conservative Republicans like Secretary of

the Treasury George Humphrey believed that excessive military spending would sap America's economic power. Indeed, leading American industrialists opposed Roosevelt's rearmament plans in 1940 because of their belief that a big military sector would distort production. It was the New Dealers who believed that military spending, far from being harmful, would actually stimulate the economy. Leon Keyserling, chairman of Harry Truman's Council of Economic Advisers, thought that as much as 20 percent of the gross national product could go to defense with no ill effects. Pump-priming by military contracts became the economic underpinning of Cold War strategy. Curiously, fiscal conservatives who today favor radical cuts in government spending in every other area to combat inflation call for sharp increases in military spending.

There is no good theoretical reason why military spending should be less inflationary than any other government spending. Indeed, as Professor Seymour Melman has pointed out, there are some compelling reasons why it is more inflationary. Cost-plus contracts drive prices up well beyond what they are in a competitive market. The beneficiaries of military contracts are for the most part highly skilled engineers, scientists, technicians, and managers whose services are in demand in the civilian economy. (Over half the nation's scientists and engineers work directly or indirectly for the Pentagon.) Personnel costs are bid up. More serious, the civilian economy is starved of innovative technical and managerial talent. The United States now lags behind every other industrial nation in the percentage of its gross national product devoted to research and development for the civilian economy. A consequence of this neglect is the competitive advantage now enjoyed by West Germany, Japan, and other smaller nations that can produce consumer goods for export more cheaply and more efficiently than can the United States.

Though the war economy has brought us inflation, technological backwardness, maldistribution of wealth, a sinking dollar, and unemployment, it is the economic drug we use to keep unemployment from becoming worse. (About 250,000 defense-related jobs were created in the recent recession through increases in the military budget.) The war economy provides comfortable niches for tens of thousands of bureaucrats in and out of military uniform who go to the office every day to build nuclear weapons or to plan nuclear war; millions of workers whose jobs depend upon the system of nuclear terrorism; scientists and engineers hired to look for that final "technological breakthrough" that can provide total security; contractors unwilling to give up easy profits; warrior intellectuals who sell threats and bless wars.

The decoupling of economic power and military power is a phenomenon of the past fifteen years. It used to be that the nations that could afford the largest armies and navies—Britain under Victoria and the Kaiser's Germany—were also the most dynamic industrial countries. (Czarist Russia with an enormous military machine and a relatively primitive industrial economy was always an anomaly.) Indeed, a spectacular army and navy was designed to symbolize great economic power. Only the richest could afford such a potlatch. But in our time two nations, one with a modest military force compared to the superpowers and the other with hardly any at all, are ascendant economic powers. West Germany and Japan are creating for the United States serious economic problems by virtue of their effective competition in the export war to which all the industrial nations of the West are committed. Exactly because they have a modest defense burden they are able to invest more in their civilian production. The Soviet Union, on the other hand, is becoming more formidable a military power but at an increasing economic sacrifice. As Cornell Professor Myron Rush notes, the heavy military expenditures are at the expense of future growth. Like the United States, the Soviets have been short-changing their civilian production machine. For the United States, the consequence has been a slow-growth economy. For a smaller and weaker economy the consequence is stagnation.

The traditional guns-or-butter debate somehow misses the point. The wish to spend scarce resources on schools, health care, the restoration of decayed cities, or clean air rather than on bombs and tanks is universal; President Eisenhower once said that to spend them on the latter when people were hungry was "theft." Nevertheless, it has been enough to silence the advocates of switching more investment from the military to essential social services to note that protection from enslavement is the most important social service a government can provide. However, excessive military spending now produces some of the same consequences as military defeat; that is, it gives foreign governments greater control over the life of the country. Take the energy crisis. The decision to invest a trillion dollars in the military rather than in a crash energy-development program to reduce a dangerous dependence on foreign oil is a prime example of increasing the nation's vulnerability by piling up hardware and expensive military bureaucracies. The hardware cannot produce energy; it consumes energy. It cannot assure access to energy, because there is no effective military strategy to assure the flow of oil through a system vulnerable to sabotage. Useless military forces preempt investment funds, public and private, that could be used to develop alternative national-security strategies appropriate to the new century which we are about to enter. Increasingly, national power comes out of innovative minds rather than the barrel of guns.

CHAPTER 6

Toward Real Security: Neither Confrontation nor Détente

The danger of nuclear war in the 1980s is awesome. Not only are inherently more dangerous weapons being built—vulnerable missiles with built-in pressures to "use them or lose them"—but nuclear weapons are being inevitably drawn into life-and-death struggles around the world. The first Cold War, we can now see in retrospect, was a relatively peaceful affair. Despite the cosmic ideological issues over which the U.S. and the Soviets occasionally threatened to blow up the world, the half-dozen men or so in Russia and America with a finger on the button never had any compelling reason to push it. The perceived need to avoid nuclear war was greater than either side's concern over the outcome of any particular confrontation.

This is not necessarily so for other beleaguered political figures of our time. The rulers of South Africa, sworn to maintain the domination of fifteen million blacks by four million whites on a black continent, are obvious customers for the technology of nuclear mass terror. Whether they actually have the bomb or, as is perhaps more likely, are in a position to acquire it whenever they wish is a detail. The threat of a nuclear Masada hangs over southern Africa as well as the Middle East.

The list of flashpoints for nuclear war is a long one. A statesman on the order of Idi Amin or some other despot with a ravaged brain; terrorist groups, with or without a cause; sophisticated criminals engaged in private-enterprise blackmail: all have plausible reasons to acquire, or to make the world believe they have acquired, nuclear weapons and the will to use them. The materials and technology for creating nuclear weapons are ever more widely available.

These developments greatly increase the likelihood of new U.S.–Soviet confrontations. In future confrontations we cannot always count on the Soviets backing down; their record of restraint in a crisis (even those they provoke) is a reflection of their relative military weakness in the past. Having achieved rough parity with the U.S. in military power, their national-security managers are now much more likely to think like their U.S. counterparts: "We can't afford to back down and be exposed as a pitiful, helpless giant." Thus the happy accident that the world has survived the first thirty-five years of the nuclear era is unimpressive evidence that we can avoid nuclear war in the coming era, for world power relationships are changing faster than we can comprehend and the arms race has become an entirely new game. The impending new stage of the military competition is likely to make the world of the 1970s look in retrospect like a Quaker village.

It is evident that in the present political climate "zero nuclear weapons" is merely a rhetorical goal, whether the rhetorician is the President of the United States or a spokesperson of the peace movement. With the spread of nuclear weapons and nuclear technology the call for physical abolition of all nuclear weapons without regard for the political, moral, and psychological changes that must accompany radical disarmament merely heightens anxiety and breeds cynicism.

Since we have long passed the point at which putting the weapons physically out of reach would make us much safer —to avoid an utterly catastrophic holocaust more than 95 percent of present stockpiles would have to be destroyed— most people have lost sight of what disarmament is supposed to achieve. Because we cannot visualize an alternative road to security except through stockpiling arms, we focus on the risks of disarmament rather than the advantages. Even the most minimal arms agreements involve the issue of transferring trust from weapons we do not understand and cannot see but believe in to shadowy foreign leaders whom we have been taught to distrust. Since the purposes of disarmament are unclear and the implications uncertain, most people prefer staying with the world we know or think we know to entering a world in which we put our trust in the sanity and decency of people rather than in the power of machines.

There has been no disarmament because the assumptions of the arms race have been almost universally accepted. Most people, including most people who favor disarmament, accept the premise that more weapons mean more security, that alternative systems of security not based on making hostages of hundreds of millions of people are utopian, and that the survival of the United States as a sovereign actor in the world justifies mass murder, poisoning of the earth, and the hideous mutation of the human species. We do not seem to be able to generate the moral passion to rid the world of arms, because we ourselves are psychologically dependent upon them.

The standard nightmare for which our national-security strategy is designed is a Soviet attack or Soviet blackmail. If we fall short of the magic number of nuclear weapons, it is argued, Kremlin leaders may think that they would suffer "only" ten million or twenty million or fifty million casualties if they push the button; they may then conclude that running the world with the United States out of the way would be worth it.

There is nothing in Soviet behavior, history, or ideology to suggest that the model of the Soviet leader waiting by the button until the computer predicts an "acceptable" casualty level is anything but a convenient fantasy to support an unending arms race. It is said that it is a harmless fantasy, a kind of insurance policy against Armageddon. But, unlike an insurance policy, the arms race directly affects the risk. By preparing for an implausible war we make other scenarios for nuclear wars—wars by accident and miscalculation—far more probable.

Anyone who ponders the elaborate system of war prevention we have erected—people in submarines submerged for months waiting for the word to destroy three hundred cities or more with the touch of a button, banks of computers that are expected to behave significantly better in communicating critical information than those that produce the billing foul-ups in department stores, cool rational leaders whom we expect to make the most agonizing decisions in a crisis without information or sleep—can understand why a growing number of scientists state flatly that if the arms race continues nuclear war is now inevitable.

What is a practical alternative for the 1980s to a national security strategy based on escalating the arms race? Arms limitation agreements can create a positive political climate in which it becomes possible to move toward an alternative security system. But only if certain requirements are met. The first requirement is that the agreement make both sides feel more secure. Since partial limitations on nuclear weapons may appear to favor one side or the other, as the opponents of SALT II have alleged, the more comprehensive the limitations the more stable the agreement. Second, the new arms relationship should have clear economic payoffs for both sides. Third, the principle of "rough equivalence" should be extended not only to numbers and characteristics of weapons systems, but to other aspects of the military relationship, including the right to acquire bases and to threaten the homeland of either power from such bases. Fourth, the explicit purpose of the agreement should be to remove ambiguities about intentions.

The more agreements require significant internal changes in both societies, the better reassurance they provide. Clear political commitment in the direction of demilitarization is not easy to reverse and thus offers the most reliable indication of national intentions. A substantially emptier parking lot at the Pentagon or at the Ministry of Defense in Moscow, or the conversion of defense plants provide a better index of national intentions even than satellite photos of missile silos, as important as they are. If the Soviets' consumer production began getting the priority attention now available only to the Soviet military-industrial complex, and their tanks began to look as dowdy as their hotel elevators, one could reasonably conclude that something important had happened. A serious program of conversion would require the leaders of both sides to confront powerful interests with a bureaucratic and ideological commitment to the arms race. That in itself would be impressive evidence of a turn toward peace.

The single most important measure toward fulfilling the four criteria I have proposed would be a mutually agreed-upon three-year moratorium on the testing and deployment of all bombers, missiles, and warheads. Such a moratorium would be verifiable by existing intelligence capabilities on both sides. During that period, the signatories would undertake to negotiate a formula for making across-the-board reductions in their strategic nuclear arsenals. The mutual moratorium, not unlike that which preceded the negotiation of the atmospheric test ban, would enable the negotiators to keep ahead of technological developments and would create a much more favorable climate for the ratification of long-term agreements.

The greatest perceived threats are not the weapons already built, although they are more than adequate to destroy both societies, but the weapons about to be built. New weapons systems convey threatening intentions. However, a freeze on all new nuclear-weapons systems would make it clear that both sides indeed intend to stop the arms race.

The Soviet Union has made a public proposal for an end to new nuclear weapons systems, although, like many Soviet proposals, it is nothing more than a topic sentence designed for propaganda effect. That it is propaganda does not necessarily mean, however, that it is not to be taken seriously. The Soviets should be pressed on their reasonable-sounding proposals.

The second element of a comprehensive framework for reversing the arms race would deal with European conventional forces and overseas bases. Geographical asymmetries have always complicated arms negotiations. The Soviet Union enjoys a military advantage in Europe by virtue of the fact that it is a Continental power and can bring its military might to bear on Europe more easily than can the United States, while the United States has a far greater geopolitical reach around the world. Although the Soviet Navy is expanding in numbers and in its missions, at this point there is no comparison between the U.S. global network of bases, ships, and alliances and Soviet capabilities for projecting military, diplomatic, or economic power at a distance. Since neither instance of military superiority can be translated into stable political power, there may be a mutual interest in trading one off against the other.

In return for a radical reduction of the Soviet nuclear threat to Europe, particularly the SS-20, which is being deployed in great numbers, the United States would agree to phase out all foreign bases now used to station nuclear strike forces capable of hitting the Soviet Union. Such U.S. forward bases are a prime example of a structure that served a function in one generation which cannot be continued in the next. As a symbol of U.S. economic and military preeminence, those bases, it could be argued, provided forms of international stability in the bipolar world of the postwar era. But that world has now gone.

Competition with the Soviets over the establishment of bases in the most volatile areas of the world such as the Middle East, Asia and Africa, and the Persian Gulf will hardly contribute to stability. Maintaining a U.S. military shield for the global array of nations we used to call the "free world" is no longer feasible. The collapse of the Shah is a good example of the inherent instability of the old arrangements based on exporting enormous quantities of U.S. military technology and stationing large numbers of Americans abroad. Since the United States finds it increasingly difficult to defend embattled regimes with military power in the face of local factors over which it has no control, the prospects for stability will depend more and more on insulating local conflicts from superpower rivalries.

It is now more important than ever before to offer an explicit, simple, and comprehensive agreement for prohibiting the further deployment of either Soviet or American military forces in other countries. We need mutually agreed-upon restriction on what each superpower can do with its military power which would outlaw future Vietnams, Dominican Republics, Chiles, Angolas, Czechoslovakias, Hungarys, and Afghanistans. We should offer the Soviets a broad agreement that embodies the principle of equality on which they have long insisted—clear ground rules which inhibit both the U.S. and the U.S.S.R. and symbolize their mutual understanding that the use of military force by the superpowers or by their proxies in the Third World is now too dangerous. Ideological competition will go on but within the confines of the new rules needed to avoid confrontation and war.

Both superpowers have much to gain by downplaying the military factor in world politics to the greatest possible extent. In an escalating worldwide arms race both superpowers will continue to lose influence as global politics become increasingly unmanageable and chaotic. The freeze on new strategic systems, the ban on proliferation of bases, base withdrawals, force reductions and redeployments in Europe make up a framework of negotiation that could lead to a significant demilitarization of the U.S.–Soviet competition. But it looks like a tall order when even modest agreements like SALT II encounter so much difficulty.

The history of recent negotiations, however, suggests that "small" agreements (they never look small to the negotiators) have a fatal flaw. Because they take a cut at one piece of the security problem, they necessarily favor or appear to favor one side. Even a minimal agreement encounters the threshold question "Can you trust the Russians?" (In Moscow read "American.") A larger package improves the chances of taking account of asymmetries of geography and military establishments, and of balancing advantages and disadvantages on all sides. Within a clear framework for reversing the arms race, risks that are unacceptable in the context of a continuing arms race become more acceptable because there is a greater payoff.

Given the realities of world power and the parallel reflex response in Washington and Moscow, there is no way out of the national-security dilemma as it is now being defined. To build a world consensus to discourage Soviet interventions, however, the U.S. must commit itself to cease further military interventions of its own. The essential characteristic of a stable relationship with the Soviet Union is clarity. An arms race never provides clarity, because any buildup of offensive forces or such an ambiguous "defensive" weapon as the anti-ballistic missile creates anxiety in the adversary, even if the weapon is procured as a "bargaining chip" for negotiation or as a counterweight to weapons on the other side. Détente, as it developed in the years 1972–79, is also too ambiguous a relationship to endure. On both sides expectations were frustrated. The Soviets received neither the massive infusion of technology and credits they had been led to expect nor the clear acceptance of their equal status as a nuclear power. The American people, having been led to believe by Nixon and Kissinger that détente was a U.S. diplomatic triumph, were surprised by the continuing Soviet buildup and the Kremlin's increasingly interventionist policy. The "principles" of coexistence were so general that they easily accommodated radically different interpretations in Washington and Moscow. The lesson to draw from the failure of détente is not that coexistence is impossible— there is no alternative—but that the terms must be spelled out in the most precise terms. Negotiators must not promise what they cannot deliver.

The U.S.–Soviet rivalry will continue. The identity of each system depends too much upon its opposition to the other to permit anything more than antagonistic collaboration between the superpowers for the foreseeable future. But there is literally a life-and-death difference between that relationship and a security system based on ever-increasing threat of confrontation. When the U.S. was running the arms race with itself, the game of nuclear "chicken" was decidedly less dangerous. The Soviets on several occasions did blink first. They have accumulated fiendish destructive power precisely to avoid being in that situation again. There is no longer a way to base U.S. security on the threat of nuclear war without running enormous risks of having to fight a nuclear war. No national-security objective can be served by such a war, for it would destroy our country and quite possibly civilization as well. America and Russia continue to stumble toward war. The greatest security threat of all is the fatalistic belief that the war no one wants cannot be avoided.

CHAPTER 7

The Foundations of American Power

The American Century lasted twenty-six years. The United States is still the largest economy, the most impressive military power, and the greatest cultural influence in the world. But we are no longer number-one nation in quite the way we once were. And we never will be again.

We have made some tragic mistakes. The greatest mistake was not to see that the extraordinary power the United States wielded at the end of the Second World War was a wasting asset, a temporary advantage which had to be used promptly to create a more permanent stability. We did not use our moment of genuine "superiority" to try to create a stable world order. We confused stability with the status quo under the belief that our sheer power could stop the clock. But in country after country changes we opposed occurred despite our hydrogen bombs and despite our dollars. The Soviet Union established its control over Eastern Europe at a moment when the United States alone had the atomic bomb.

The decline of American power was no doubt accelerated

by our mistakes, most notably the war in Indochina, but it would have occurred in any event. The unique circumstances at the end of the war that gave us that power were bound to change. Indeed, it was our policy to make them change. We are in the evening of the American Century. Does this mean that the sun is about to rise on a Soviet Century?

Almost certainly no. The Soviet Union, with a larger population and an economy half the size, is still an underdeveloped country. It has enormous internal problems. The non-Russian "minorities" are about to become a majority and will create increasing problems for the Great Russians who run the Kremlin. The economy is stalled, and the very legitimacy of the system is in question. The Soviet model is admired nowhere. Soviet-supported military intervention has increased, but Soviet influence has ebbed dramatically. It is worth remembering that the Soviets' influence in the world depends more on what other countries do than on what they themselves have so far accomplished. Russia's popularity was high at the end of the Second World War because Stalin, despite his own desperate deals with the Führer, symbolized the radical alternative to Hitlerism and the decadent capitalism of the 1930s. It rose again during the Vietnam War when the Soviet Union could capitalize on being the ally rather than the destroyer of a little country under attack. Soviet influence in the world is far more a function of Western failures than of socialist success. West Europe's increased readiness to trade with the Soviet Union is a consequence of reduced fear of Russian intentions, not panic. The Soviets have had the physical power to ruin Europe ever since the 1950s.

But the Soviet Union is a formidable military power, and it is becoming more of one. Does this mean that the Soviet Union will use force to expand its empire and its influence? Soviet ideology categorically rejects the idea of expansion by military force. The Soviets talk a great deal about the "correlation of forces," but this is as much a political and economic concept as a military one. The Soviet leaders are aware of the danger of war and of the catastrophic consequences of war. Their fear of intensified pressure from the West is genuine. Despite their greater capacity to project military power, they are more isolated politically than they have been for many years. With the exception of France, there is hardly a Communist party other than in a client state or an occupied country which supports them—and there too there is increasing tension. More than a hundred nations condemned the U.S.S.R. after the Afghanistan intervention. Every nuclear missile in the world not in the Soviet Union or on a Soviet ship, their generals point out, is aimed at the Soviet Union. The Soviets' instinct is to try to exert tight control in any situation where they perceive an interest. But they are aware that military power is not easily translated into political control. Eastern Europe lies under the heel of the Soviet Army, but Soviet control is uncertain. If the Soviet Union cannot successfully occupy Eastern Europe, how could it successfully occupy Western Europe, even if the attempt could be made without risk of nuclear war?

The Soviet Union is most likely to commit aggression under two circumstances. The first is that it senses its own security slipping away and makes a military move, as in Afghanistan, to stabilize its shaky domain. The more the Soviet Union feels its relationship with the U.S. is unstable, the more likely it is to make such a military move. The second circumstance in which the U.S.S.R. might well use military power is where the temptation to do so is overwhelming because of the political vulnerability of the U.S. The U.S. should therefore build situations of strength, but the source of such strength is not more military hardware but strong political relationships. We need a much clearer definition of the national interest in the Third World and a much closer collaboration with the rest of the industrial world on new rules for developing a just international economic order. Our failure to project power is due to our preoccupation with military strategies that cannot work and our insufficient attention to political and economic strategies that can work.

We are fated to live in a century of turmoil to be dominated by no single nation. For a brief moment the United States played a traditional imperial role. Our model was nineteenth-century Britain. We explicitly took over "responsibilities" as they slipped from British hands. By the time the American Century was over there were 150 nations, several revolutions in military technology, and an evolving world economy that made it impossible for any nation to play the old role of world policeman. It is the fate of the Soviet Union to have come to world power at a moment when the nature of power has changed and the era of imperial opportunity has passed.

The new century will not resemble the old. The distribution of power will be much more diffuse. We are entering a time of increasing danger, but the source of the danger is different from what it was in Hitler's time or what it was in the Cold War. A national-security strategy for the United States in the 1980s must start with the world as it is. It cannot be based either on utopian dreams or on paralyzing nightmares.

If the United States is to reverse the decline in its power and security, we must recognize that the uncontrollability of the arms race is the greatest threat we face. War is not a national-security option in the nuclear age. If our strategy for war prevention fails, everything fails. Whether the survivors number in the millions or the tens of millions, the American experiment will be over. In thirty minutes we will have cashed in two hundred years of history and, perhaps, put an end to all history.

The decline in power to control our destiny should indeed worry us, but it has nothing to do with a lack of nuclear hardware. It stems from an increasingly uncontrollable international environment in which the superpowers increasingly risk being sucked into other people's wars. It stems also from a failure to manage our society. Nothing could restore American prestige and influence faster than a dramatic reduction of our foreign oil dependence and a workable approach to the management of inflation that did not tear the country apart. Our influence in the world is directly related to our ability to confront successfully unprecedented problems of advanced industrial society and to create a legitimate social order within the limits of a slow-growth economy.

National security must be based on national power. But the nature of power has changed, while our strategy has not. The only basis of national power is a stable international order. Such an order cannot be imposed by any nation. It can be constructed only by the cooperative efforts of many nations. The United States is dependent on other nations, particularly our European and Japanese allies, in new ways because of their new power. So also Mexico, Nigeria, and other resource-producing nations. Mass misery in the Caribbean and in Central America is no longer just a humanitarian problem. The waves of immigrants from desperately underdeveloped countries are transforming the character of American society and the very nature of the national interest.

The most crucial elements of power are a strong economy and a strong spirit. The revolution in military costs forces difficult choices. In a time of austerity, increasing the military budget while the domestic programs are being slashed raises the issue, not of guns versus butter, but of missiles versus the local police and firefighters. The distortion of priorities has become so acute that as the Administration counsels a massive increase in military spending, essential services in every major American city are being cut. To suggest that the threat of "finlandization" in Europe is a greater threat to the people of Chicago, Cleveland, Los Angeles or Detroit than the loss of social services, the breakdown of the education system, the rise in crime, the alarming increase in infant mortality, the impending municipal bankruptcies, the failure to invest in appropriate alternative energy systems or to revitalize American industry is to distort the meaning of "strength."

War will come about only if we lose the spirit and the will to survive. The whole purpose of modern war is to demoralize the enemy population. But we now run great risk of demoralizing ourselves. Even if nuclear war never comes, the psychological toll on our people is enormous. A recent poll in California revealed that 85 percent of the respondents expect a nuclear war and about an equal number believe that they will not survive it. Exactly how this awesome threat affects child development, family life, and the rise of an uncharacteristic mean-spiritedness in our political arena cannot be calculated. But living for two generations under the shadow of the bomb has taken its toll. The realization that we are all thirty minutes away from catastrophe and that we and the Russian people are hostages for the political behavior of leaders neither of us can control saps our spirit and paralyzes constructive action. If this country ever bows to a foreign country it will be because we have defeated ourselves, not by learning the facts of nuclear war but by losing the hope, courage, and imagination to avoid it. France vintage 1940 rather than contemporary Finland is the historical example that ought to concern us. The greatest army in Europe surrendered because the society it was defending had rotted.

Our peculiar national problem has always been isolationism. In the postwar decade we defined isolationism as an unwillingness to use our military power to bring stability to the world. But isolationism manifests itself in other ways. A nation can live with such nostalgic illusions of power that it closes its eyes and stops up its ears. It was not amusing to read in the *Washington Post* the headline "CIA TO STUDY ISLAM" at the very moment there were three million people in the streets of Teheran. Our spiritual isolation has cut us off from the major currents that are now transforming power in the world. Our isolationism also threatens to cut us off from our closest allies now that they are exerting a degree of independence unknown in the brief American Century. Isolationism feeds dangerous self-deception. We begin to believe that our agenda is the only one that matters to other people. But strange agendas are now appearing all over: wars over languages we never heard of, over different ways to worship Allah, over battles fought thousands of years ago. If we wish to exert power in the world we will have to be far more sensitive to agendas we cannot control.

The great historic movement of our times is not Communism or socialism but revolutionary nationalism in a variety of forms. We have set ourselves an impossible task by defining U.S. national security to mean that we must control political change in the Third World. Our official reasoning for supporting military dictatorships with a narrow political base in Asia, Africa, and Latin America has not changed since the time of John F. Kennedy. "There are three possibilities in descending order of preference [the President was considering what action to take in the Dominican Republic]—a decent democratic regime, a continuation of the Trujillo regime [a bloody dictatorship] or a Castro regime. We ought to aim at the first, but we really can't renounce the second until we are sure we can avoid the third." We fear the triumph of socialism in other countries so much that we continually tie the national destiny to doomed regimes and undermine our own legitimacy as a force for freedom and democracy in the world.

It is ironic that at the very moment the Soviet Union has

lost much of its ideological force the United States is reviving ideological diplomacy. In El Salvador and South Africa, to name two instances, the U.S. is aligning itself with a Right that is ultimately doomed in order to stave off a victory of the Left. The Carter foreign policy appeared to be a vacillating one because it alternated between this classic U.S. position and a new realism. Within days of assuming office the Reagan Administration tried to revive the politics of the American Century. Military aid to a murderous junta in El Salvador was stepped up and the trickle of U.S. military advisors grew. The "falling dominoes" rhetoric of the Vietnam era was revived, and U.S. allies, some of whom saw more hope for long-term stability in the revolutionary forces than in the increasingly desperate generals, were enjoined to fall in behind the leader of the Free World. At the risk of alienating the principal regional powers, Mexico and Venezuela, the United States was once again committing its prestige to a regime whose only strategy of survival was to make war on its own people.

Under Carter the new realism had won out in Nicaragua and Zimbabwe. Neither society is a paradise, but neither represents a threat to the United States or a triumph for the Soviet Union. Exactly because our power is not what it was and the world is changing fast we had better keep our eye on our vital interests. The United States can, and indeed it must, live with a variety of political experiments in the Third World. Socialism in Latin America, especially if it comes about by a popular movement or a democratic election, is not a threat to the United States. Every nationalist regime of the Left that has come to power in the Western Hemisphere has preferred to do business with the United States and to receive aid from the United States rather than relate to the Soviet Union—for obvious reasons. Even a country as ideologically aligned as Vietnam has sought a posture of diplomatic nonalliance based on a commercial and diplomatic relationship with both the United States and the Soviet Union.

Every regime of the Left in the Third World is in trouble, but then so is every regime of the Right. It is legitimate to argue about what development model makes sense for underdeveloped countries, but it is foolhardy for us to try to settle the argument for them by sending in the Marines or the CIA. For one thing, our ideological friends often hurt us more than our putative "enemies." The Shah of Iran did us far more damage than Castro can ever do. Second, a victory for a radical nationalist regime does not make the Soviet Union more of a threat. The success of revolutionary movements outside Russia—even when the revolutionaries call themselves Marxists and even when they hang Brezhnev's picture on their walls—is not necessarily a victory for Russia. It does not add automatically to the power of the Soviet state. It is usually a financial drain. The more heavy-handed the intervention, the more likely the revolution is to slip away from Soviet control. Indeed, it is now clear that independent revolutions represent liabilities and threats to the Soviet leadership. Today, with China on one border and an explosive Eastern Europe on the other, the Soviet Union is the only nation in the world virtually surrounded by hostile Communist powers.

Revolution is neither pretty nor necessarily successful even in its own terms. Moderate alternatives in the direction of a just society in desperate countries are preferable, but they are not always possible. The longer the United States asserts as its national interest the prevention of revolution, the more it will advertise its impotence and give openings to the Soviet Union it would not otherwise have. Instead of assuming that the Soviet Union is responsible for radical political change around the world and abandoning radical regimes to the Soviet camp, our policy should be to have correct and, hopefully, friendly relations with countries struggling to meet the basic needs of their people. They may fail. The odds are not encouraging. We may not like their methods. A dictatorship of the Left is no more attractive than a dictatorship of the Right. But why should a dictatorship of the Left which sets as its priority health care, literacy, land reform, and equality of opportunity be an automatic "enemy," and a dictatorship of the Right that exercises power in behalf of a few landowners and industrialists be an automatic "friend"? In any event, we should try to separate as much as possible the U.S.–Soviet military confrontation, which is our most serious security threat, from internal political struggles in the Third World, which do not pose threats to our security, whatever the outcome. This means that neither superpower should have a military presence. The inevitability of radical change in desperate countries on the brink of starvation or in the grip of murderous governments ought to be obvious, but it by no means follows that revolutionary governments should be pro-Soviet. We would do better to be guided by history instead of Soviet propaganda on this point.

There is panic and violence in the world—not, as at other historical moments, because of a fanatic belief that one system or another has a monopoly on truth, but because of widespread feelings that no one in charge knows what to do. The failure of both "socialist" and "capitalist" regimes to bring liberation or dignity to billions of people has unleashed in many parts of the Third World a profound spiritual reaction—a radical rejection of the dominant international culture.

The object of national security is to protect people and to make them feel secure. But as the nation adds to its nuclear stockpile our peoples' faith in themselves and their future is sagging. President Reagan has pronounced the economy a "mess." Our education system is a shambles, a clear indication of our inability to invest in the future. The threat to

life and property in the United States from crimes of violence mounts daily, and neither walls, locks, missiles, tanks,
guns nor electric chairs will lift the burden of fear. Nostalgia
for lost power that can never be recovered is no basis for
security; the mindless accumulation of weaponry is sapping
the spirit of our people. The power that can make us secure
is not the power to bend other nations to our will, but the
power to remake an America that is once again committed
to the values for which the nation was founded—justice,
opportunity, and the liberation of the human spirit.

If we could learn that uncontrollable forces of liberation
are on the move in the world and that they need not be our
enemies, we could help to create a political climate in which
aggression can be contained. To develop the strength to act
in the world so that our children and grandchildren may live,
we will have to rebuild our faith in the possibilities of a
decent society—not just for ourselves but for our four billion
neighbors. More missiles or aircraft carriers will provide neither that desperately needed political hope nor practical political options. The real danger in a dark and turbulent time
is that we scare ourselves into impotence, and perhaps obliv-
ion, because we have forgotten why we became a nation.

Bibliography

Books

Aldridge, Robert C., *The Counterforce Syndrome: A Guide to U.S. Nuclear Weapons and Strategic Doctrine.* Washington D.C.: Institute for Policy Studies, 1978.

Angell, Norman, *The Great Illusion,* 2nd ed. New York: G. P. Putnam's Sons, 1933.

Barnet, Richard J., *Intervention and Revolution.* New York: New American Library, 1972.

———, *The Giants: Russia and America.* New York: Simon & Schuster, 1977.

Business Week, The Decline of U.S. Power (and what we can do about it). Boston: Houghton Mifflin Co., 1980.

Blechman, Barry M., and Kaplan, Stephen S., *Force Without War: U.S. Armed Forces as a Political Instrument.* Washington D.C.: The Brookings Institution, 1978.

Kaplan, Fred, *Dubious Specter: A Skeptical Look at the Soviet Nuclear Threat.* Washington D.C.: The Institute for Policy Studies, 1980.

Melman, Seymour, *The Permanent War Economy: American Capitalism in Decline.* New York: Simon & Schuster, 1974.

Podhoretz, Norman, *The Present Danger.* New York: Simon & Schuster, 1980.

Tuchman, Barbara W., *The Guns of August.* New York: Bantam Books, 1976.

Monographs and Articles

Aspin, Les, "How to Look at the Soviet Military Balance," *Foreign Policy,* spring 1977, No. 22.

———, "Judge Not by Numbers Alone," *Bulletin of Atomic Scientists,* June 1980.

Barnet, Richard J., "Challenging the Myths of National Security," *The New York Times Magazine,* April 1, 1979.

————, "U.S.–Soviet Relations: The Need for a Comprehensive Approach," *Foreign Affairs,* spring 1979.

Center for Defense Information, "Soviet Geopolitical Momentum: Myth or Menace?" *The Defense Monitor,* vol. 9, no. 1, 1980.

Cox, Arthur Macy, "The CIA's Tragic Error," *The New York Review of Books,* Nov. 6, 1980.

Kennan, George F., "The Sources of Soviet Conduct," *Foreign Affairs,* July 1947.

————, "U.S.–Soviet Relations: Turning from Catastrophe," *Christianity and Crisis,* May 26, 1980.

Klare, Michael, "Have R.D.F., Will Travel," *The Nation,* Mar. 8, 1980.

LeoGrande, William M., "Cuba's Policy in Africa, 1959–1980," monograph, *The Institute of International Studies,* University of California, Berkeley, 1980.

Pipes, Richard, "Why the Soviet Union Thinks It Could Fight and Win a Nuclear War," *Commentary,* July 1977.

Seligman, Daniel, "Our ICBMS's Are in Danger," *Fortune,* July 2, 1979.

Tonelson, Alan, "Nitze's World," *Foreign Policy,* fall 1979, no. 36.

Warnke, Paul C., "Apes on a Treadmill," *Foreign Policy,* spring 1975, no. 18.

Government Documents

U.S. Department of Defense, *United States Military Posture FY 1975.* Washington D.C.: Government Printing Office, 1974.

————, *United States Military Posture FY 1981.* Washington D.C.: Government Printing Office, 1980.

————, *Annual Defense Department Report FY 1981.* Washington D.C.: Government Printing Office, 1980.

Unpublished Sources

Sanders, Jerry Wayne, Peddlers of Crisis: The Committee on the Present Danger and the Legitimation of Containment Militarism in the Korean War and Post-Vietnam Periods, Ph.D. dissertation, University of California, Berkeley, 1980.

Index

121